"COME LEARN OF ME"

"COME LEARN OF ME"

Spiritual Object Lessons

By
Derek Arthur Sharpe

XULON PRESS

Xulon Press Elite
2301 Lucien Way #415
Maitland, FL 32751
407.339.4217
www.xulonpress.com

Cover design and watermarks by Kimberly Lewis

Editing Assistance by Dr. Carmielle Wilkerson

Unless otherwise indicated, Scripture quotations taken from
the King James Version (KJV) – *public domain.*

Dictionary references unless otherwise noted are from
Webster's 1828 Version.

Printed in the United States of America.

ISBN-13:978-1-54565-668-6

Table of Contents

Dedication

There were not a variety of options as I prayerfully contemplated to whom this book would be dedicated. There was only one. My parents, Arthur Sharpe, Jr. and Marian Lois Sharpe have been the instruments in God's hands to shape and mold me into a vessel of righteousness from the moment I was born. They have faithfully modeled before me all that is just, righteous, and good. Of course, they are not perfect; of course, they made mistakes, but I can confidently declare before God and man that all the good in me is because of them. There is no man on this planet that I hold in higher esteem than my father. There is no woman on this earth who has a higher place of honor in my heart than my mother. Through their lives, their words, their joys, their sorrows, their reactions to adversity and trial, I have received the template for coping with all that life sends my way. In their own separate and unique way, each has shown me what dependence and reliance upon Jesus truly means. If there is any good in me, if there is anything positive that can be said about me, it is because of God working through the instrumentality of my parents. I owe all I am to them. They have shown me consistent, unconditional love each day of my existence. The Lord allowed my mother to pass on October 4, 2018. She did not get to hold this book in her hand and that is a regret that I will keep in my heart always. I praise the Lord that my father, by God's grace, will be able to see and read these words from my heart.

God Himself has commissioned me to write this book. By His grace and in His strength, I have completed the task. Its goal is to go far and wide and teach others of Jesus' will, His way, and His love.

My precious, precious parents, my daddy and my mommy, I dedicate this book and all the lives that it will touch to you, the wind beneath my wings, the root of all I am. I love you with all my heart. Your son, Derek Arthur Sharpe

Foreword by Angela Sharpe

The bell rings. It is the first day of school. I timidly enter a classroom. I am stunned. This classroom is unlike any other I have ever walked into–it has no books, no paper, no pencils, no desks, no computer, and no chalkboard. How and what will I Learn? A voice is heard, "Welcome, you have come to learn of Me." The Master of all, the Ultimate Teacher, begins to unfold His carefully designed curriculum. It is as though, like a book, the world peels open in His hands as He begins to select teaching tools, or might I say, instruments of salvation. These are the animate and inanimate objects surrounding us daily in our challenged world. They are the vast variety of all nature that testify of Him, their Creator. They are the illustrated, unforgettable stories from the Bible that demonstrate the unconditional love and forgiveness of God. Then finally, the instructors known as the eight talents, which are given to all mankind, will leave deep impressions of God's amazing wisdom in giving us daily reminders of who He is as they accompany us throughout our life.

They have all been chosen to educate the minds of men to the ways, the will, and the love of God through His creative works. Each object lesson is an illustration of the spiritual blessings given to those who desire to be connected to God. The instructions are clear: Listen! Listen! Hear what you see!

Under inspiration the author has captured the blueprint of God's lesson book and pattern of teaching. It was not just Jesus' words that captivated an audience in classrooms by the seaside or in the open field, but it was His compelling style of teaching in using commonly observed and used objects.

One chapter from the book of Jesus' ministry of miracles, shows Him opening the eyes of a blind man. The man's eyes slowly peel open, and looking up he saw *"men like trees walking."* This divinely orchestrated lesson was selected with our author in mind, for he has been to me. . .a man *"like a tree"* walking.

As the wife of the author, I have been honored to live beneath the surface of this man of God's life. Behind closed doors as it were, under the earth, hidden from view, is where respect for the foundation of a tree is gained. I have been blessed to dwell among the roots of his private experiences. It is commonly known that it is the root of the tree that truly determines the nourishment of the fruit. I have been privileged for 30 years to watch, like no one else, the development, cultivation and the consistent progress of spiritual roots growing deeper and deeper through every trial and victory in his life. It is said, *"a tree is known by its fruit."* As many others, I have sampled the fruit produced by his connection to God. The undeniable ripening of his character has revealed that God has continuously poured into his soul the nourishment of disappointment and faith, defeat and courage, forgiveness and humility, and love and peace., so that all who would partake of his ministry would benefit and be blessed.

Like his parents who were dedicated educators, the author traveled the path of higher learning throughout his life—from teacher to principal to pastor. In essence, "The Classroom" has become his "Dressing Room." He allows God to daily prepare and strengthen his root system through earnest prayer, consistent deep study of the Word, and a faithful lifestyle. Whether our author stands in a classroom or a pulpit or even before his precious souls in his Nursing Home Ministry of 14 yrs., God has given him the gift to transform earthly illustrations to heavenly principles through Spirit-filled messages that are designed to clothe each hearer with the beautiful foliage of Christ's righteousness. From the shores of Maine to the mountains of Montana and even to the island of Fiji, many have been converted and encouraged to give their hearts to God and to enter a greater knowledge of His Way of holiness through practical everyday encounters.

Because the author sincerely seeks to live what he preaches and teaches as a Pastor and husband, my own spiritual roots have been deepened and fortified in Christ. The author's love for God and style of teaching has influenced and greatly impressed my style of learning and teaching as a Christian and as a teacher. This book has opened my mind to the lengths that God is willing to go to communicate His message of love and salvation to man. All nature testifies to the character of God. Everything that He has made and every object that exists, every concept formulated, and even life itself has been drafted in the Master's hand as a teaching tool to convey the thoughts of God.

As parents, teachers, pastors, leaders and "regular" people like me, our goal is not just to be rooted and grounded in Christ, but to become more and more **fruitful. This** book will assist you. As you matriculate through the pages of this book, prepare to grow higher, grow deeper, and grow wider.

Now Beloved, sit still and be still. Class is in session. The Master Teacher approaches the podium of life. A voice is heard, "Come Learn of Me!" Please, "Come" know Me....

Introduction

An object lesson according to *Merriam Webster's Online Dictionary* is "something that serves as a practical example of a principle or abstract idea. A lesson taught (especially to young children) using a familiar or unusual object as a focus."(1) The *Grammarist* elaborates:

> Dictionaries define an object lesson as something that serves as a real-world example of an abstract idea or principle. The term comes from the educational practice of using a material object to help illustrate the abstract ideas of a lesson. But in actual sense, the phrase's definition is often closer to a concrete example of why something should or should not be done a certain way.(2)

Stated another way, An object lesson uses that which is familiar to introduce that which is unfamiliar; it uses what people know to aid their understanding of what they do not know. The principle does not necessarily have to be abstract, but merely not known. There is much that is concrete, touchable, tangible that many individuals just have not been exposed to. This is the methodology that the greatest teacher to ever walk this earth utilized in planting in the minds of His pupils the principles and concepts that would impact and mold their lives forever. That teacher was Jesus Christ of Nazareth, the Saviour of the world.

When Jesus walked upon this earth, preaching and teaching and healing, there were always lasting lessons to be learned, precious gems to be garnered, and spiritual principles to be absorbed. His life was a pattern and a guide and for those who were impressed and led by the Holy Spirit, the object lessons that could be gleaned from His life and ministry were infinite. Proverbs 4:18 informs us that "the path of the just is as the shining light that shineth more and more until the perfect day". This scripture reveals that as life continues, there will be deeper truths revealed, broader principles explained, higher precepts grasped. This is the nature of Divine inspiration. It cannot be exhausted. It cannot be mastered. No matter how much one has already gleaned from a subject, there is still more that the Spirit can and will unveil to the surrendered mind, to the humble and teachable heart.

Jesus began teaching long before He walked this earth as the carpenter from Nazareth. When He spoke this world into existence, He created a living classroom overflowing with lessons to instruct His people in the ways of righteousness, the ways of holiness, in short, the ways of God. The sky with its sun, moon, and stars is His white board upon which He traced eternal principles that would stimulate the most astute minds. The vast oceans, the forests teeming with living creatures and luxurious greenery accented with splashes of colors only an infinite Creator could have contrived, are waiting to share the truths that the Sovereign of the universe has authorized them to impart. The animals, wild and domestic, the fish and the fowl, all have heavenly license to share the ways and operations of God to any student with a willingness and hunger to know more about their Creator. Even the earth itself with its mountains straining towards the heavens, canyons that declare eternal insights and revelations that connect the dots in ways heretofore unimagined, have been commissioned by God to declare their Maker's praise to all who will listen. All of creation is a divinely accredited institution of learning, beckoning to all as did its Creator – "Learn of Me."

This book is our Heavenly Father's attempt to bring greater focus and attention to the God-ordained teachers and instructors that many in the body of Christ have never even known to exist. For others it will be a shedding of greater light upon subjects already known, but in which only the surface has been scratched as it relates to the lessons that God so fervently longs for His people to experience. It is the purpose of this book to bring every person who reads it that much closer to experiencing the divine injunction and invitation of Philippians 2:5 – "Let this mind be in you which was also in Christ Jesus." Nature's primary purpose is to aid us in gaining deeper insights into the ways and mind of God. As we grasp God's glory, God's character, God's way in and through nature, we are better able to view everything in this life through the eyes of Christ, with the mind of Christ which allows us to then see, as we have never seen before, the myriad of Heavenly object lessons that surround us.

The book is merely a signpost pointing its readers in a direction. The concepts presented herein will not by any stretch of the imagination be comprehensive in their nature. You are about to embark upon a journey that will never end.

Throughout the ceaseless ages of eternity, you will *still* be gaining broader, higher, and deeper insights and revelations into the ways of God through His creatures and His handiwork.

The educational journey upon which you are about to embark cannot in the truest sense be compared to any earthly educational system or institutional curriculum. Isaiah 55:8,9 reminds us that "His ways are not our ways and His thoughts are not our thoughts." Although there will be similarities and familiar phrases employed as it relates to education, the courses you will experience, the teachers who will instruct you, the homework given, even the sequence of the classes, will be different from what is done here on earth. Dispense with all expectation of something familiar and come with an open mind and an open heart to be instructed in an entirely new way, by entirely new teachers, on possibly entirely new concepts.

This book is divided into three course offerings: There will be eight examples given through the classroom of nature. Eight lessons drawn from the day to day activities and objects that are a natural part of our surroundings, and finally, we will be taught from the greatest book that has ever been written – the Bible, the divinely inspired word of God.

We will approach these course offerings from a different perspective that will allow us to embrace who Jesus is, how He operates, and the Divinely destined part you, dear reader, have been called to play in making that which is unfamiliar *familiar*. Again, the Spirit is inviting you, "come, learn of Me."

<u>Nature</u>

As we begin this classroom journey, as with any other course, there is a textbook. The textbook for this class is the Bible, also known variously as "The Word," "The Holy Scriptures," or the "Sword of the Spirit." Unless otherwise noted, all scripture references will be taken from the King James Version. Feel free to use another version if it does not hinder your comprehension of the concepts presented. The very first classroom that God placed man in was nature. No desks, no chalkboards or white boards. There were no walls, no bulletin boards, (at least not as we perceive them to be), but the Garden of Eden was indeed a classroom.

Let us keep in mind that the entire purpose of this classroom journey is to learn of Christ, His ways, His will, His perspective or point of view as it relates to how a thing truly is, which ultimately embodies His love. With that thought in mind, the very first concept that we will learn is that God does not make suggestions. If He says it, He expects you to do it, if you want to pass the class. That means when we encounter such words as "consider" or "let" we are being given a classroom assignment and *all* assignments are expected to be "turned in" one way or another. Sometimes just comprehending and receiving the concept is all that is required from the Master Teacher. He is a gracious and merciful instructor. Let us see some places in our textbook that give us clear indication that the environment in which the first human pair was placed was full to overflowing with instruction. Psalms 19:1 states, *"The heavens declare the glory of God and the firmament sheweth His handiwork."*

In a later chapter we will deal more fully with the fact that the "glory of God" means the "character of God" or the "way of God."

When we hear Christ as our instructor telling us the "additional reading" we need to do to "learn of Him," we need to pay attention and "do the homework assignment." In Job 12:7,8 Christ points us to some additional teachers that can explain to us in more detail just who God is and how He operates. Listen closely to the instruction. Our teacher is literally instructing us to attend additional classes:

7 But ask now the beasts, and they shall teach thee;
and the fowls of the air, and they shall tell thee:
8 Or speak to the earth, and it shall teach thee: and
the fishes of the sea shall declare unto thee.

Remember, our Divine Instructor does not make suggestions. We were instructed to ASK the beasts and they will
TEACH us. We were further instructed to *ask* the fowls of
the air and they will *tell* us. We were admonished to *speak*
to the earth and it also will *teach* us, and finally, *If* we *asked*
or *spoke to* the fishes of the sea, they as well will *declare*
something to us. What will they teach and declare? Who
God is, how He operates, His mind, His character, His way.
This is what your Heavenly Instructor is teaching you at this
very moment. Listen attentively, take notes if you need to
– "My way is in all things, animate and inanimate. My way
is found in them. They are My preachers. They bring forth
My messages. They yield themselves to be My teachers, My
messengers." That instruction is in quotations not because it
is from any book, but because that is your Instructor talking
to you. Those are not my words; they are His.

We need to see this instruction from another perspective,
so we will turn to our textbook. Once again, we are going
to undergo a paradigm shift or a change in mindset. How
WE define words is usually *not* how God defines words. We
will now prayerfully consider Matthew 19:17. It says: *And
he said unto him, Why callest thou me good? there is none*

good but one, that is, God: but if thou wilt enter life, keep the commandments.

We just received a powerful principle. Did you get it? Allow me to explain what the above scripture did *not* say. Jesus was not saying why are you calling *Me* good because *only* God is good, so *please* do *not* call Me good. That would mean Jesus was declaring that *He was not God*; therefore, He should not be called *good*. John 10:30 teaches "*I and my Father are one.*" We receive further enlightenment in 1 John 5:7 which reiterates this principle by stating, "*For there are three that bear record in heaven, the Father, the Word, and the Holy Ghost: and these three are one.*" In Matthew 19:17 Jesus was asking the inquirer whether he understood the implications of how he had just addressed Jesus. He had called Christ "Good Master" and Jesus was "instructing" the man that the only personages who could be called *good* were *divine*. What is the vocabulary lesson we just received? From God's perspective, the word "good" means Godly, heavenly approved of at a level that is higher than human. Keep in mind, we are learning all of this, so we can better accept that we just learned that God's way is in everything He has created.

Now that we have a better grasp on God's definition of the word "good," let's see if God called anything else "good." In the first two chapters of Genesis we hear God calling *everything* that He created in the first five days *good* and on the sixth day after He created man, He declared it all to be *very good*! Let us pause and digest what we just learned. God's way, God's character was implanted, instilled, inscribed upon *everything* that He created in those six days! Every tree, every flower, every animal, every fish, every star, the sun and the moon, ALL were individually qualified and authorized to teach who God is. Unfortunately, sin entered this world and it made it more difficult to learn the lessons from the teachers, *but they have never stopped teaching*! The rest of this section will be dedicated to allowing the Holy Spirit to teach us how to pull the Divine object lessons out of eight different teachers in the classroom of nature. They will help us to learn more of Christ, His way, His will, His love.

The Thorn

I was not part of God's great plan,
His words did not include me.

When all was done in those six days,
there were no thorns to see.

The first couple could enjoy a rose
without my hindrance there.

No prickly briers, nor thistles sharp,
just beauty everywhere.

But then one day, one fateful day, everything was changed.

God's creation was impacted, the symmetry rearranged.

An intruder entered God's pure world,
came right in through the door,

Ushered in through selfishness,
an unreasonable longing for more.

More than what God had provided,
more than the absolute best,

When faced with the great temptation,
our first parents failed the test.

The atmosphere's now tainted,
there's a chill in all the earth.

Gone is the joy that mankind shared,
replaced by an eerie dearth.

This is how I came to be, I am an amalgamation.

A metamorphosis born from sin an enemy to creation.

Now the beauty of the rose is accompanied by the thorn

A new environment now exist, a paradox is born.

Derek Arthur Sharpe

The Thorn

Ｔhe thorn is an object in the world of nature. It was
not, however, a part of God's original creation. It
is a result of sin, a consequence of transgression. It is not
the handiwork of God, but an intruder introduced by our
great enemy. But God, in His infinite power and wisdom,
has chosen to use the thorn as one of His instruments. As
one inspired writer has stated, "The same God who guides
the planets works in the fruit orchard and in the vegetable
garden. He never made a thorn, a thistle, or a tare. These
are Satan's work, the result of degeneration, introduced
by him among the precious things; but it is through God's
immediate agency that every bud bursts into blossom."(3)
Genesis 3:17, 18 teaches us that the thorn was introduced
to man *for his benefit* after he forfeited his right to be in the
educational institution known as the Garden of Eden. The

earth would *still* be his teacher, but some of the lessons–*for his benefit*–would now be accompanied by pain: Thus, our introduction to the thorn:

> *17 And unto Adam he said, Because thou hast hearkened unto the voice of thy wife, and hast eaten of the tree, of which I commanded thee, saying, Thou shalt not eat of it: cursed is the ground for thy sake; in sorrow shalt thou eat of it all the days of thy life; 18 Thorns also and thistles shall it bring forth to thee; and thou shalt eat the herb of the field;*

There is a three-word phrase within this lesson that if missed, destroys the entire lesson our Divine Instructor would have us learn. *"For thy sake."* Adam did not receive a curse. The ground received the curse and the curse was a *blessing and a benefit* to Adam! It is within this context that the thorn is introduced. Its purpose – to bring blessings out of curses, joy out of sorrow, healing out of pain, triumph out of defeat. It is only when we truly grasp this critically important and vital foundational principle that we can see through the eyes of our Maker, God's character in the thorn. God's way of dealing, His operational procedure in His

Divinely authorized teacher – the thorn. A thorn is generally viewed as a burden, an annoyance, a necessary evil, but God is not an arbitrary God. He is not capricious or whimsical. He does not do things just to do things. He *is* a good God. If He allowed it, there is a *good* reason and purpose for its existence. Besides the human application of the thorn, there is another reason for the thorn, the spine, or the prickle. "In plant morphology, thorns, spines, prickles, and in general spinose structures are all hard structures with sharp, stiff ends, generally with the same function of physically deterring animals from eating the plant material. In common language the terms are used interchangeably, but in botanical terms, thorns are derived from shoots(so they can be branched or not, they can have leaves or not, and they arise from a bud). Spines are derived from leaves (the entire leaf or some part of the leaf that has vascular bundles inside) and prickles are derived from the epidermis(so they can be found anywhere on the plant, and don't have vascular bundles inside so they can be removed more easily than thorns and spines)."(4)

What did we just learn? In nature, God uses the thorn, the spine, the prickle, as a deterrent, a protection, a defense mechanism. And often, as in the case of the rose, beauty is the result of the thorn playing its role effectively.

Legend states that there is a tiny creature known as a thornbird. The thornbird spends its entire existence seeking and searching for the perfect thorn and when it finally finds the perfect thorn it impales itself on that thorn, wounding itself to the death. As the thorn pierces its breast, guaranteeing that its life will soon be over, the thornbird brings forth the most beautiful song – a melody that cannot be surpassed in beauty, a melody that cannot be brought forth any other way than by a pain that results in death. This song above all songs can only be produced by a thorn.

From this lesson we should *never* look at the final scenes of our Saviour's life the same. When those cruel, unfeeling Roman soldiers placed that crown of thorns upon our Saviour's head, little did they realize that, like the thornbird, the Saviour had lived His entire life for *that moment*. Comprehend the scene as He experienced the *piercing* of the thorns, and the *piercing* of the nails in His flesh, the *piercing* of the splinters from the rough-hewn cross, and most excruciatingly, the *piercing* of a people, a church, a nation that had forsaken Him, even down to His most beloved twelve Apostles. It is in this context that we grasp the object lesson of the thorn. It was the *piercing* that brought forth the most beautiful song that humanity *will ever hear, "It is finished!"*

It was the *piercing* that brought forth that song that insures us an opportunity of eternal life. As the Saviour's life ebbed away, He sang some music before the final stanza that applies to us all. *Through and despite* the piercings He sang a song to John the beloved to take care of His mother. To the forsaken and deserving of death thief on the cross, He sang a song of acceptance and salvation. To a countless number of misguided and deluded Jews who had participated in His death, He sang, "Father, forgive them, for they know not what they do"(Luke 23:34).

This, dear reader, learner of His way, is what the piercing of the thorns produced: A song for the ages. A song of victory. A song of deliverance. A song of assurance. It was the thorns that kept Christ focused on His mission. It was the pain that prevented the enemy of His soul from gaining access to His mind. Yes, the purpose of the thorn is to protect, to instruct, to save. The Bible tells us that Paul had a thorn that he asked God to take from him, but 2 Corinthians 12:7-9 tells us that Paul's thorn was serving a Divinely instituted purpose. The pain and weakness of the thorn was the mechanism Christ was using to make Paul strong! There is strengthening in the piercing! Listen attentively to the lesson of the thorn:

7 And lest I should be exalted above measure through the abundance of the revelations, there was given to me a thorn in the flesh, the messenger of Satan to buffet me, lest I should be exalted above measure.

8 For this thing I besought the Lord thrice, that it might depart from me.

9 And he said unto me, My grace is sufficient for thee: for my strength is made perfect in weakness. Most gladly therefore will I rather glory in my infirmities, that the power of Christ may rest upon me.

Please learn this most vital lesson. The purpose of the piercing is to bring strength through humility, acceptance, and utter dependence upon Divine aid. The enemy of our souls has produced a counterfeit piercing. Instead of humility, it brings attention to self. Instead of acceptance, it declares that I answer to only myself. Instead of dependence on God, it asserts all I need is within myself. We must always be on the lookout for the counterfeit piercing. The fundamental object lesson of the thorn – it *is* for man's sake and if humbly submitted to and received, it will make us strong and give us an opportunity to sing in death, the death to self, the most beautiful melody of salvation and victory that we have ever learned.

From this point on in your life, when you see a thorn, see your Saviour on the cross, enduring the piercing for you. *This* is God's way. It is His will. It displays His love. Victory can only come through suffering. Our Saviour suffered for us, that we could experience eternal life. It is God's way to bring us low in preparation for exaltation. See God's character in the thorn. It is His way to take that which was meant for evil and use it for good. He gives each of His precious children a wonderful promise found in Romans 8:28. In summary it teaches us that no matter how bad, how awful, how trying, how debilitating, how humiliating, how life changing, it WILL, it MUST work together for your good! The thorn teaches us the wonderful principle that what the enemy of our souls has crafted and designed for our pain and destruction, God uses that very thing to bring us joy and bring glory and honor to His Precious Name. Learn of Me. It's His way.

Lessons from the Thorn:

- Uncomfortable things can be beneficial.
- Blessings can come out of curses.

- God is not an arbitrary God. Everything He does/ allows has a good purpose.
- Adversity is often the instrument God chooses for protection.
- That which pierces, strengthens.
- Humility is the only true preparation for exaltation.
- We are at our strongest when we realize our utter help-lessness and place our total dependence upon God.
- Jesus' life and death teaches us that it is His way and His will and His love that true victory can only be obtained through suffering, for it cultivates humility and gratitude.

Seasons

Recurring faithfully year by year,
displaying a myriad of views,

Pure driven white, a deep burnt orange,
a collage of never ending hues.

They come, each one, always on time,
punctually reporting for duty,

Declaring for all who see and hear,
that God Himself loves beauty.

They teach us lessons of faith and trust,
that though the way is dark and drear,

This too must pass, it cannot stay,
no matter what, the end is near.

The bloom of Spring declares so sweet,
He does make all things new.

He is a God of second chances, He does indeed love you.

The Summer, with its harvest rich,
proclaims God does provide,

In Him there is security, In Him we all can hide.

The falling of the leaves so fair,
show beauty amidst the sorrow,

Its scenes of grandeur unsurpassed,
place hope within tomorrow.

And even Winter's barren cold reveals the Master's plan,

It is through death that God Himself brought life to every man.

This never ceasing cycle, this train of events so fair,

Combine to teach one lesson- God is always there.

Derek Arthur Sharpe

Seasons

The seasons are another tremendous teacher in God's Divinely appointed educational institution. Like the thorn, they were not a part of God's original educational curriculum. After sin, and especially after the flood, the seasons emerged as instructors in the school of Christ. At the onset of this course, it is interesting to note that there is no such thing as an everlasting season. The very essence of the word means a beginning and an ending. The first lesson we learn from the seasons is the faithfulness of God. From the moment that seasons came into existence, they have continued in unvarying order for almost six thousand years. *That* is the unvarying, unchangeable *faithfulness* of our Heavenly Father. Through the object lessons of the seasons we *know* that we can *trust and rely* upon God. The seasons encourage us to have faith in God. E.G. White had this to say regarding seasons.

> God's works in nature have lessons of wisdom and gifts of healing for all. The ever-varying scenes of the recurring seasons constantly present fresh tokens of His glory, His power, and His love. Well were it for older students, while they labor to acquire the arts and learning of men, to also seek more of the wisdom of God, – to learn more of the divine laws, both natural and moral. In obedience to these are life and happiness, in this world and in the world to come. (5)

What are some additional object lessons that our Divine Instructor would have us glean from the seasons? First, each season has a specific purpose and a specific time. Certain things can only happen in a specific season. Ecclesiastes 3:1 states: *To everything there is a season, and a time to every purpose under the heaven:*

The Bible teaches us that *everything* has a season or a TIME OF DURATION. This is the way our Saviour operates with man during this *season of sin*. I want to repeat that so you can praise the Lord in your very soul! *Sin is seasonal*!

Unlike our Heavenly Father who has *always been and always will be*, sin had a beginning point and will have an end! Praise God! One of the fundamental differences between the kingdom of God and the kingdom of Satan is that God's kingdom has no end, but Satan's kingdom will pass away! The Bible refers to Satan's kingdom as "the world." Notice how 1 John 2:15-17 accentuates the difference between the two kingdoms:

15 Love not the world, neither the things that are in the world. If any man love the world, the love of the Father is not in him.

16 For all that is in the world, the lust of the flesh, and the lust of the eyes, and the pride of life, is not of the Father, but is of the world

17 And the world passeth away, and the lust thereof: but he that doeth the will of God abideth for ever.

The scripture shows us all that is in the world is not of the Father, but is of the world– Satan's kingdom–and then it gives us reason to rejoice in saying "the world passseth away and the lusts(desires) thereof, but he that doeth the will of God abideth forever OR has no ending, therefore, *no season*! This, indeed, is cause for celebration, but just like the thorn, while the seasons are here, we must inquire, how do we allow them to draw us closer to God and instruct us in His ways?

The seasons teach us that we must learn to look for the indications. None of the seasons just abruptly come upon us. There are gradual indications that give those who are paying attention *time to prepare for the upcoming season.* The seasons of our lives are cyclical. All of us have a spring, summer, autumn, and winter cycle in our lives. Our lives will be richly blessed by allowing the Holy Spirit to show us (1)what season we are currently in; (2) what things need to be done or can be done in this season, and (3) finally, what are the *indications* that will show us when to begin preparing for the next season.

During Jesus' life on this earth, He was constantly being asked to do things that it was not time for Him to do. It was not His season. There came a time during His ministry when the disciples along with the people wanted to crown Him King, but it was not time for Jesus to be crowned King, so he had to distance Himself from the people(John 6:14,15). At various times during His ministry, the Jews attempted to kill Jesus, but it wasn't time for Him to die, so the Jews were unable to carry out their murderous plans. But when the *season* came, the Bible says Jesus "set His face towards Jerusalem" because He knew it was *His time*"(Luke 9:51).

Many times, we attempt to accomplish things in our lives and we cannot follow through because we are not in the correct season for those things to take place. We must allow the Holy Spirit to give us the insight on what can be accomplished and when. It is important to note a very critical lesson that our "Seasons instructor" teaches clearly–*seasons are cyclical*! No one is in Winter forever AND no one is in Summer forever. If things are going wonderfully for you right now, take advantage of the season *and* watch and pray that you will be able to discern the *indications* that will show you when your season of plenty is coming to an end. That is why the principle of preparation is such an important part of the classroom of Seasons. God *commanded us as students* to take another class from one of His teachers called the ant. Pay close attention to the season/preparation principles that are taught by God's tiny instructor: We will prayerfully "consider" Proverbs 6:6-8. Look for the seasonal/preparation principles:

6 Go to the ant, thou sluggard; consider her ways, and be wise:

7 Which having no guide, overseer, or ruler,

8 Provideth her meat in the summer, and gathereth her food in the harvest.

We are told to consider or learn from the ways of the ant. She provides or does what is needed in the Summer, so she can reap a harvest in the Fall, so she can have what she needs in the Winter. In our lives, there is something specific that we need to be doing at that time. We cannot know it on our own. We must be connected to the Holy Spirit, so He can lead, guide, and direct us. The ant can do it without a guide or overseer because all of nature is still completely obedient to the will of God. Only man has *chosen* to step outside of God's will and therefore must make special effort to reconnect with God's will and God's way. Until Jesus comes again, each of us, if faithful, will experience the entire seasonal cycle repeatedly. If things are not going well for you right now, the lesson from the Seasons is that there is a divinely prescribed time of duration for your hard time. The critical point that God wants you to remember, dear reader, is that sometimes a person is not *ready* to leave their winter because they have not made the necessary preparation to be able to sow or as the ant, "provide" in the Spring and Summer, and therefore they pass through the seasons that were supposed to enable them to prosper, and find themselves facing another winter unprepared. Throughout Scripture we are admonished to "watch and pray"(Matthew 26:41, Mark 13:33, Luke 21:36, Colossians 4:2, 1 Peter 4:7). This admonition is certainly a "Seasons instruction." If we do not recognize the signs, then we will be out of position when the test or the opportunity presents itself. Malachi 3:6 reminds us that God does not change. He alone is unchangeable. Everything else has a season and a reason or purpose. Nature teaches us through the seasons to watch, prepare, and stay connected. Our Divine Instructor invites us to learn of Him, being alert, being ready, being in tune with Heaven, this is His way, His will, and His love.

Lessons from the Seasons:

- God's faithfulness is unchanging, unvarying, always dependable
- Everything in life has a specific duration, a specific purpose, and a specific time for occurring.

- Sin is seasonal. It will not always be
- God's kingdom has always been and will always be. Satan's kingdom has only been in existence for a short time and will soon cease to exist forever.
- We must learn to identify the indications that prompt us to prepare for the upcoming season
- Seasons are cyclical. No one and nothing stays in the same condition forever
- Preparation is essential for progress
- Preparation must be accompanied by prayerful watchfulness and attentiveness
- Jesus' life teaches us that we must, through the guidance of the Holy Spirit, do the things we are supposed to accomplish at the appropriate time or they will not produce the Divinely desired results
- Reiterated, Christ's life shows us that we must only do or say that which it is time to do or say when it is time to do or say it. Timing is an essential element of God's will, His way, and His love.

The Butterfly

Delicately wafting on the waves,
sublimely flittering through the air,

Serenely oblivious to all around,
going through life without a care.

Bringing joy to all who see,
adding beauty where ere it lands,

There is so much it does not know,
most things it cannot understand.

And yet it glides so gracefully,
making the best of every day,

Sharing its message of hope and cheer in its
own magnificent way.

It knows of struggle, it knows of pain,
the butterfly knows well the fight,

Indeed, without the last great battle,
it would not have the gift of flight.

From flower to flower, from tree to tree,
searching for the nectar's scent,

To look for all that's beautiful is how this
little creature's bent.

It comes in numerous tints and hues,
in so many shapes and sizes,

The wonder and delight brought forth it never even realizes.

For all who have an ear to hear this is the
lesson that is taught,

Before you fly, before you soar,
there is a battle that must be fought.

You must wait, you must start low,
patience holds the perfect key

That unlocks the door and brings you forth for all within the
world to see.

Derek Arthur Sharpe

The Butterfly

D elicately beautiful, wonderful to watch as they effortlessly fly from place to place, what are the principles that our Divine Instructor would have us partake of and digest from this tiny educator from Heaven's hand? What spiritual object lessons could possibly be derived from this tiny creature with a lifespan ranging from a month to a year depending on various factors? As we are slowly learning how to view things from our Maker's perspective, let us again put down our own limited human understanding and reasoning and allow the Holy Spirit to grant us the ability to pay attention and learn the lessons that God has commissioned the butterfly to teach us, and as we do so, we will be that much closer to learning of Him, His way, His will, His love.

The butterfly's life consists of four basic stages- The egg stage, the caterpillar stage, the chrysalis stage, and finally the adult stage. There are, of course, a wide variety of object lessons that we can learn from the butterfly, but for our purposes here, we will allow our butterfly instructor to share three fundamental object lessons. The first lesson we learn from a Spirit-led study of the butterfly is the all-important principle of humility. All throughout the Bible the necessity for humility is emphasized over and over. James 4:10 admonishes us to *"Humble ourselves in the sight of the Lord and He shall lift you up."* 1 Peter 5:6 reminds us to *"Humble yourselves therefore under the mighty hand of God, that he may exalt you in due time."* Matthew 23:12 declares *"And whosoever shall exalt himself shall be abased; and he that shall humble himself shall be exalted."* One of my favorite scriptures teaches that humility is a requirement for effective praying. If we are not humble before God, there is really no need for us to believe that our prayers are accomplishing what we would like them to accomplish. Prayerfully pay attention to the Divine steps that are outlined in the following passage found in 2 Chronicles 7:14. Remember, it is a Heaven-ordained sequence. It *cannot* be done outside of the prescribed order of the Sovereign of the Universe. Listen carefully - "*If my people, which are called by my name, shall humble themselves, and pray, and seek my face, and turn from their wicked ways; then will I hear from heaven, and will forgive their sin, and will heal their land.*" You will notice that it is humility that begins the process that culminates in healing. How exactly are we to learn this lesson of humility from this tiny little creature? We must study its beginnings. Once it comes out of its egg, the butterfly grows into a hairy, fuzzy caterpillar. Some have remarkable colors and markings, but for the most part, they are hairy, fuzzy worms. All they can do is crawl around from place to place and they are not even that efficient at doing that. At this point in their existence they are not supposed to be doing a lot of traveling. Their purpose is to get on a leaf and eat it up and go to the next leaf and eat it up and so on. While we are learning this lesson of humility, we want to make sure we don't miss the lesson that we often get ourselves into difficulty because we are attempting to do something that it is not time for us to do. Our butterfly instructor will have more to say on that a little later. Now, the butterfly is the lowest of the low, crawling from place to place. Vulnerable to attacks from predators with absolutely no defense mechanism other than camouflage *If* it stays in the proper environment.(Did we catch that lesson?), the fact that it will one day be floating serenely in the air isn't very encouraging. The butterfly teaches us that we all must crawl *before* we walk *or* fly because *that* is God's way of dealing with His children who are afflicted with the malady of sin. To go high before going low is the perfect recipe for a disaster. Only humility can truly handle the heights.

The next lesson we glean from our fragile friend is patience. The butterfly(which is a caterpillar now, not resembling a butterfly *at all*) has its current phase and still one more uncomfortable phase to endure before it can float throughout the skies, a wonder to all that behold it. This is where patience becomes an excellent attribute. Without it, we make foolish mistakes that could even be life threatening. James 1:4 says it best - *"But let patience have her perfect work, that ye may be perfect and entire, wanting nothing."* Hebrews 12:1 coaches us that we must "run with patience the race set before us." 1 Peter 1:5-8 describes a Divinely prescribed ladder that each child of God must climb, by God's grace and in His strength. Patience happens to be the rung immediately preceding *godliness*. So, when we allow God to perfect patience in our individual lives, we are then, and only then, ready to enter the classroom of godliness.

This is an extremely important lesson that we cannot afford to miss from our Heaven-sent educator. Without patience the chances are high that we will do something and abort the entire process! Faith is a factor as well because it is our belief and trust that God does indeed have a plan for our lives, even if we haven't the slightest idea *what* it is or *how* we will ever achieve it while in our current condition. Remember, the butterfly is currently a hairy, fuzzy, crawling, worm and from this stage it goes into a chrysalis.

There is a possibility that some of our students that have enrolled in Butterfly 101 do not know what a chrysalis is. Let me enlighten you. It is a jail cell. It is a coffin. It is a strait jacket to the tenth power. It is complete and total confinement with absolutely *no room to move*. This is where the butterfly finds itself. Shut off from the rest of the world. Not even able to crawl at this point (so it truly would appear that the process has taken a step backwards) the butterfly/caterpillar is now a prisoner.

Patience is truly the answer at this part of the journey. Job had a chrysalis experience. He talks about it in Job 23:8-10. See if you can hear him describing the chrysalis.

8 Behold, I go forward, but he is not there; and backward, but I cannot perceive him:

9 On the left hand, where he doth work, but I cannot behold him: he hideth himself on the right hand, that I cannot see him:

10 But he knoweth the way that I take: when he hath tried me, I shall come forth as gold.

Did you see it? Nothing forward, nothing backward, nothing to the left, nothing to the right, a really trying place to be. What was Job's response to the chrysalis? God knows what is going on. He is in control of the process and when this process is complete, *I shall come forth exactly the way God ordained for me to come forth*! I believe our dear brother Job had been an exceptional student in a butterfly class somewhere. Now the caterpillar is undergoing some outstanding, tremendous changes while in this chrysalis. It is becoming a butterfly. No one can see that it doesn't look like a hairy, fuzzy caterpillar any more. The caterpillar cannot even see that it doesn't look like that anymore. But it must be able to sense and feel that despite the awkward and seemingly troubling environment that it has found itself in, something good is happening.

Now for the final lesson for now from Professor Butterfly. The chrysalis finally begins to split. The *butterfly* begins to emerge from its chamber of confinement. But it does not have an easy exit. The butterfly must exert an enormous amount of effort just to get out of the chrysalis. At times, it seems as if it just is not going to get out.

I have been asked by our instructor to share a story I heard with you: There once was a man who was walking in a garden and he happened upon a butterfly struggling mightily to emerge from its chrysalis. The man was kindhearted and immediately went to the aid of the struggling butterfly and broke open the chrysalis, so the butterfly could emerge. As he opened the chrysalis, the butterfly fell helplessly to the ground. Its wings were wrinkled and disheveled. It crawled around on the ground striving to spread its wings and enter the air, it's Divinely appointed destiny, but it was not to be so. That butterfly would wander around on the ground for the rest of its life. Why? Because the strengthening of its wings was in the struggle to get out!

Dear student, we cannot help but catch the twofold lesson that is being taught! Sometimes we try to help someone, but because we are not connected, because we cannot hear the Holy Spirit telling us *not to help*, we do immeasurable, sometimes irreparable, harm. All in the name of trying to help! Proverbs 14:12 gives us the sober admonition - *"There is a way which seemeth right unto a man, but the end thereof are the ways of death."* But back to the primary lesson from our butterfly instructor – The struggle is Divinely ordained! It is a critical part of the process! Pay attention to how the Apostle explains it in 1 Peter 5:10 -

"But the God of all grace, who hath called us unto his eternal glory by Christ Jesus, after that ye have suffered a while, make you perfect, stablish, strengthen, settle you." Did you see the struggle? After you have suffered *a while* did not give the connotation of something short-lived. And the rest of the process did not seem like anything especially easy. Paul counseled Timothy in 1 Timothy 2:3 to *"endure hardness like a good solder."*

Even Jesus Himself gave this sobering instruction in Matthew 24:13, *"But he that shall endure unto the end, the same shall be saved."* Almost doesn't count. The final lesson the butterfly teaches us is if you are going to fly, if you are going to truly fulfill your divinely appointed destiny on this earth, you are going to have to fight, to struggle, to press through, until you break through. Endurance and perseverance are the final lessons of this class. Christ is humble. We must be. He is patient. We must be. He endures to the end. We must endure to the end as well. Will you, dear reader/student, learn of Him? He will never leave you nor forsake you. This is His will, this is His way, this is His love. The classroom of the Butterfly has come to an end.

Lessons from the Butterfly:

- Humility is essential to all true success.
- Often failure is the result of attempting to do something it is not time to do.
- We all must crawl before we walk or fly because that is God's way of dealing with His children who have been infected by sin. It is beneficial to the process.
- Patience is essential to any successful process.
- The Bible refers to patience as the perfecter.
- Impatience often aborts the entire process.
- Faith is an essential element in trusting God when it is unclear what is going on.

- The struggle is what gives you the strength to fly.

- Often, we do more harm than good when we give unauthorized assistance.

- No matter what, we must endure to the end.

The Wind

Whispering sweetly, scarcely discerned,
meandering softly through the trees,

Gently bending the flowers fair, tickling with an invisible breeze.

Shouting with a thunderous roar, striking terror in all who hear,

Shattering all within its path, wreaking havoc, causing fear.

Nature's paradox, kind, but mean,
God's conundrum, keeps us guessing,

In His mighty, stretched out arm, it can bring a curse or blessing.

Humans cannot see the wind, only God can trace its form,

He alone can point it out in the restless, raging storm.

It can be our friend or foe, refreshing on a Summer's day,

Soothing with its gentle touch in a wondrous, welcomed way.

But it can mangle what we love, completely decimate all we own,

Leave us helplessly distraught forcing us to weep and moan.

A symbol of the Holy Spirit as well as bloodshed, war and strife,

Its weaved into the very fabric of this thing we all call life.

Within the realm of God's creation, the wind does truly have a place,

Revealing chapters of His mercy and His never-ending grace.

Derek Arthur Sharpe

The Wind

It is a daily part of our lives. Where we live, the type of life we lead, the type of work we do, all have a bearing on how often we encounter the wind. It is always near. How can the wind be one of our Divinely anointed instructors? How do we learn from something we cannot even see? Are you ready? We will now be introduced to the Heavenly facilitator of this next course of instruction – the wind.

The first thing we must do is get accustomed to recognizing our teacher in our textbook. He is always there. We just must be in tune, connected, in the right place or mindset to see Him. The wind is God's vehicle of choice. The Lord rides in the wind. The Lord speaks through the wind. The wind is God's conduit for the Holy Spirit. Notice how your textbook begins: Genesis 1:1, 2:

1 In the beginning God created the Heaven and the earth.

2 And the earth was without form, and void; and darkness was upon the face of the deep. And the Spirit of God moved upon the face of the waters.

Did you see Him? The Spirit of God moved upon the waters. It was in the wind! Can we find him in other locations of the Bible? Acts 2:1-4

And when the day of Pentecost was fully come, they were all with one accord in one place.

2 And suddenly there came a sound from heaven as of a rushing mighty wind, and it filled all the house where they were sitting.

3 And there appeared unto them cloven tongues like as of fire, and it sat upon each of them.

4 And they were all filled with the Holy Ghost, and began to speak with other tongues, as the Spirit gave them utterance.

We again see the wind being used as the vehicle to house the Holy Spirit. Notice its effects were something that could be *seen* and *heard*. Please comprehend this vital principle.

Whenever we encounter the wind, we should be looking for and listening for the Holy Spirit. God wants us to learn the power of the wind. When we see it, be it gentle or fierce, we must grasp completely that God Himself rides on the wings of the wind. God's breath is in the wind. He blows softly or tremendously, but it is His breath. He speaks to His people through the wind. He so fervently wants us to learn to hear Him. The wind has *power*. Even a soft gentle breeze can do many things! The object lesson is this: It doesn't have to be forceful to be powerful! A gentle breeze can alter attitudes, change moods, give strength to carry on right now when a person is about to give up. The soft gentle breeze can turn one's attention to God, prompt a person to reflect upon the goodness of God, remind someone of the wonderful things God did for them in the past. Why? Because it is God Himself, speaking through the wind, shaping and molding the mindset of each heart that is tuned to the frequency of Heaven. THIS is the lesson of the wind. It is the wind that allows the eagle to soar gracefully and effortlessly upon its airwaves and the message our Divine Instructor wants us to receive each time that we see a bird soaring serenely through the air is that our Heavenly Father desires to allow us to soar through life the same way. Allowing the wind of His Holy Spirit to lead and guide and direct us far above the complexities and anxieties of life. The wind represents God's power to redeem a soul from sin, to alter a course bound for destruction and reset it for a course of life and life more abundantly. When we see the wind, we recognize that we are not actually seeing the wind. We are observing the effects of the wind. Like the Holy Spirit, it is invisible, but the impact it has upon a life, it can and will be seen in every precious soul that surrenders to the promptings of the Spirit. One author articulated it thusly "While the wind is itself invisible, it produces effects that are seen and felt. So, the work of the Spirit upon the soul will reveal itself in every act of him who has felt its saving power. When the Spirit of God takes possession of the heart, it transforms the life. Sinful thoughts are put away, evil deeds are renounced; love, humility, and peace take the place of anger, envy, and strife. Joy takes the place of sadness, and the countenance reflects the light of heaven. No one sees the hand that lifts the burden, or beholds the light descend from the courts above. The blessing comes when by faith the soul surrenders itself to God. Then that power which no human eye can see creates a new being in the image of God."(6) Thus, we see the power of the wind. But our Heavenly Father also speaks through the wind. When the sun is blistering hot and there is no shade to be found, the gentle, refreshing breeze that comes is God whispering "I love you. I care about the little things as well as the big things. Your comfort is important to Me."

How many times have we not responded when Jesus was speaking to us? We must learn the lessons the wind is seeking to teach us. But not all of God's messages are pleasant ones. God speaks through tornadoes, hurricanes and tempest. There are times when the waywardness of man must be addressed, and God uses the wind to convey His displeasure. It is at these times when we must look within ourselves and examine our lives to see if there is anything there that would cause our Heavenly Father to speak to us in this manner. The Bible depicts God speaking in a still small voice and in peals of thunder. Consider the following passages found in 1 Kings 19:11,12 and Exodus 20:18.

11 And he said, Go forth, and stand upon the mount before the Lord. And, behold, the Lord passed by, and a great and strong wind rent the mountains,

*and brake in pieces the rocks before the Lord; but
the Lord was not in the wind: and after the wind an
earthquake; but the Lord was not in the earthquake:
12 And after the earthquake a fire; but the Lord was
not in the fire: and after the fire a still small voice.*

Did you learn that lesson dear students? Sometimes God
will use the wind to break down the obstacles and hindrances
in your life that are preventing us from being able to hear
Him. He not only uses the wind, but He is also more than
capable of using His other created elements to remove the
strongholds that are distracting us and preventing us from
hearing Him. The fire, the earthquake, are as equally at His
disposal as is the wind. But when they have accomplished
their purpose, make no mistake, it is the wind, the soft, gentle
breeze that carries the still small voice of the Spirit.

*18 And all the people saw the thunderings, and the
lightnings, and the noise of the trumpet, and the
mountain smoking: and when the people saw it, they
removed, and stood afar off.*

This is the verse that comes immediately after the Ten Commandments that the people heard God speak from the mountain. It describes God's voice as "thundering" and as the noise of a trumpet. The lesson we must learn is God determines HOW He wants to speak to us. No matter whether it is loud or soft, it is in our best interest to pay attention. There is one final lesson we must learn from the wind. There are indeed times when our great adversary, the devil, is granted permission to use the wind and the destruction that follows is the work of his hand, not that of our Heavenly Father. Only those who are connected to God will be able to discern whether it is God or the devil using the wind. Our textbook provides us a wonderful account that allows us to know that even when the enemy is using the wind against God's people, God Himself CAN and WILL come in and use His overriding authority. In Mark 4:35-41 we see that Jesus had received a call from a precious soul that was in bondage, shackled in Satan's darkness and despair, possessed beyond measure, a plague to society, a castaway, living among the tombs. Satan heard the call and saw Jesus responding to the call and summoned the winds to destroy the boat where Jesus and the disciples were located on the sea of Galilee. The disciples panicked because the boat was sinking, and the wind was buffeting them, but where was Jesus? Getting some much-needed rest! SLEEPING IN THE STORM! Why? How? Because Jesus knew that He was the Creator, the Master of ALL CREATION and that the wind could not do anything against the will of its Master! Can you see it students? Are you capturing the picture in your mind's eye? The wind that Jesus created, the wind that Jesus used to speak, to comfort, to break down and build up, that wind is apparently destroying the vessel where Jesus is sleeping, all so a soul in darkness will not be set free! When Jesus is rudely awakened out of His sleep, He is not bothered, He is not frustrated at the complete lack of faith of His disciples. He addresses their concern and simply says what only the Master of the Universe can say to a howling, raging, destructive wind – "Peace, be still." And just like that the wind goes away! Why? Get the lesson dear reader, because the wind belongs to Jesus! It is His wind, His vehicle. Every time you see the wind from this time forward, let it teach you, let it remind you. This is God's way, He comes as it is necessary to come, as the situation and circumstances dictate that He come. He may breathe on you with a soft, gentle breeze or He may arrest your attention with a thunderous storm. Either way, it will be God speaking to you-displaying His will, His way, His love. Make sure that you pay attention. Another lesson has been taught by a Divinely authorized teacher of Righteousness.

Lessons from the Wind:

- The wind is God's vehicle of choice.
- The wind is God's conduit for the Holy Spirit.
- Something doesn't have to be forceful to be powerful.
- We must tune our hearts to listen and hear the messages God speaks to us in the wind.
- God also uses the wind to break down and destroy the obstacles that prevent us from hearing Him.
- Only those connected to God will be able to discern whether it is God or the Devil using the wind.
- God speaks both in a still, small voice as well as in thundering, trumpet tones.
- Whether or not God is speaking in a still, small voice or in a loud thunder clap, it is in our best interest to pay attention to what He is saying.
- Because Jesus is the Creator, He will always be the Master of the wind.
- If Jesus allows the Devil to use the wind, we can trust that God has a plan.

The Mountain

Silently it stands in grandeur, a majestic, mighty tower
Speaking without using words, of its strength and untamed power.
Whether it be snowcapped white or luxuriant green and flourishing
Stark and barren as a desert or full of life, so kind and nourishing.
Of this edifice of nature, one thing is so very clear,
In this realm of architecture, no human hand has entered here.
There is no man who has the blueprint, none can truly make this claim
All the glory, all the honour, points alone to God's great Name.
Straining, stretching, pointing upward towards the heavenly
courts above,
Declaring loudly, boldly singing of the Master's wondrous love.
Never budging, never shifting, it can't be pushed out of its place.
Immoveable, recalcitrant, defying all from peak to base.
Climb it, scale it, paint its picture, strive to capture all its wonder,
All who do will be compelled to stop and question, pause and ponder.
Who is the author of this mountain, what mighty power am I seeing?
The only answer- the Creator, Lord of all, the Supreme Being!

Derek Arthur Sharpe

The Mountain

Massive in size, awe-inspiring in grandeur and majestic beauty, the mountain is indeed a Heaven-appointed teacher of righteousness. The very first lesson you must learn about the mountain is that only God can make a mountain. Mountains are "God-formed." If man made it, it is not a mountain. The Bible teaches us that mountains were "brought forth." Listen to how the psalmist explains it in Psalms 90:2:

Before the mountains were brought forth, or ever thou hadst formed the earth and the world, even from everlasting to everlasting, thou art God.

That is such interesting terminology. Brought forth, *The New American Standard Version*, *The New Living*

Translation, as well as the *English Standard Version* translate or paraphrase it thus: that before the mountains were "born." *The Living Bible* states, before the mountains were "created." Capture that lesson in your mind. Write that concept upon the notebook of your heart. Mountains were *born, they were created, they were brought forth* for a Divine purpose. What lessons can we learn from this silent giant of a teacher? We must understand what a mountain represents. Each time we see a mountain, our minds should be drawn to worship our Creator. Mountains are symbols of the dwelling place of God!

Come with me as we take a short journey through the scriptures and allow the word of God to aid us in learning this lesson from our Mighty Instructor in the ways of God. Remember, every one of these verses will be pointing us to the fact that mountains represent God's dwelling place, His House, His Tabernacle, His church, His Pavilion. Prayerfully consider the following:

Psalms 3:4, *I cried unto the Lord with my voice, and he heard me out of his holy hill. Selah.*

Where was God when He heard your prayer? He was in His holy hill.

Psalms 15:1

Lord, who shall abide in thy tabernacle? who shall dwell in thy holy hill?

Here, we see the Bible using the "state, restate" format. First, we see the phrase using the words "abide" and "Tabernacle," and then we see the exact same phrase repeated substituting "dwell" and "Holy Hill." God refers to mountains as His holy hills and as His tabernacles.

Psalms 99:9

Exalt the Lord our God, and worship at his holy hill; for the Lord our God is holy.

God now adds the dynamic of worship in His Holy hill. Why? Because God is there, and He is holy!

Isaiah 2:2

And it shall come to pass in the last days, that the mountain of the Lord's house shall be established in the top of the mountains and shall be exalted above the hills; and all nations shall flow unto it.

Here we see the mountain being referred to as the Lord's house. The place where He dwells. Are you beginning to see it?

Isaiah 56:7

Even them will I bring to my holy mountain and make them joyful in my house of prayer: their burnt offerings and their sacrifices shall be accepted upon mine altar; for mine house shall be called a house of prayer for all people.

Wonderful dynamics are being added for our benefit. Not only is the mountain HOLY, it is also referred to as my house of prayer.

Every time we see a mountain, it is telling us to pray, it is telling us to worship, it is telling us to remember that God Himself dwells in the high and lofty places. Psalms 121:1 says *I will lift up mine eyes unto the hills from whence cometh my help. My help cometh from the Lord which made Heaven and earth.* That was a powerful lesson we just learned!

David said he looked to the hills for help. He then went on to add that it was not the hills that were helping him. It was the Lord that was his help. Why did David include the hills? Because the hills were the dwelling place of the Lord! Mountains represent the presence of God and when we see them, we should reflect upon His faithfulness, upon His Holiness, upon His creative power.

There is another lesson that we can learn from the mountains if we allow our giant teacher to instruct us. Listen closely. Every mountain is a place of praise. Because God is there, praise *must* be there as well. Mountains are reminders that we should stop what we are doing and praise the Lord!

In algebra there is a formula that states if a= b and b= c, then a= c. Let us apply some Divine principles to this formula. Psalms 113:5 states that God dwells *on high*. Isaiah 57:15 states that God dwells on high *and* He inhabits(or dwells or lives) in eternity. So far, we have (a) God inhabits or dwells on High and in eternity. Psalms 22:3 teaches us that God dwells in the *praises* of Israel. Now we have all the pieces of our Divine formula that our Mountain Instructor is striving to teach us. If (a) God inhabits or dwells or lives in the High place of Eternity and (b) God inhabits or dwells or lives in the praises of Israel, then (c) The high places or mountains are places of praise! When we see mountains, they should cause us to praise the Lord because that is where He lives and that is what He expects! Praise from His people. Worship from His people. Prayer from His people. Truly, the high and holy mountain teacher has been commissioned from the foundation of the earth to instruct God's people in His way, His will, and His love.

The final lesson that we will learn from the mountain is that God is faithful. He never changes. Man cannot move a mountain. They are placed there by God Himself and they stand as testimonies to His unchangeable nature, His unwavering love, His reliable protection. When we see the mountain, we see security. We can rest in His love, for truly He is our refuge and strength, a very present help in trouble (Psalms 46:1). One author has painted this portrait of the mountain's ability to bring comfort to the soul in these words: "The mountains that girded their lowly valleys were a constant witness to God's creative power, and a never-failing assurance of His protecting care. Those pilgrims learned to love the silent symbols of Jehovah's presence." (7) Truly this Divine instructor has given us object lessons of the way, the will, and the never-changing love of our Creator and Saviour. May we always keep close to our hearts, the instruction we have received from the mountains and continue to accept the plea of our Saviour to "Learn of Me."

Lessons from the Mountain:

- Only God can make a mountain.
- Mountains are symbols of the dwelling place of God.
- Mountains instruct us to worship God.
- Mountains remind us to pray to God.
- Mountains declare that our help comes from God alone.
- Mountains motivate us to praise God.
- Mountains testify to the faithfulness of God.
- God is unchanging, unwavering, completely reliable.
- Mountains represent the security that can be found in God alone.
- Man cannot move a mountain, and neither can man move God.

The Tree

Arms outstretched in praise and worship, admiration within each leaf.

Covering, shadowing, providing comfort for all
who would come beneath.

Some are bending, some are stalwart, some stay green
and some grow bare.

In this world where ere you travel, you will find them standing there.

In the tundra of the arctic, underneath the desert's sun.

In the teeming concrete jungle, in the fields where rivers run.

Bringing forth a wide assortment, fruits and nuts that cause delight,

Some can make you pause in wonder at the beauty of their sight.

Starting as a tiny seedling, growing to a massive tower,

Standing through all sorts of weather, showing strength
and untold power.

In each tree there is a story, it matters not how small the start,

If you persevere and struggle, if you try with all your heart,

If your roots are deep and sturdy, if the ground you're in is good,

You will grow and flourish greatly as a tree that's growing should.

Then you will fulfill your purpose, then you will become a tree.

Doing what the Master tells you, standing tall for all to see.

Derek Arthur Sharpe

The Tree

The tree is overflowing with object lessons! It has been used in Scripture for so many applications in both the natural and the spiritual world. By God's grace we will enter the classroom of the tree acknowledging that it, too, is a Divinely authorized instructor of Righteousness. If we pay attention and allow the Holy Spirit to lead and guide our understanding, we will continue on our journey of accepting our Saviour's invitation and command to "learn of Me.

The very first lesson the tree desires to teach us is that we cannot limit God as to how He will use us! There are a wide variety of things that the tree can be used for and it is not the tree's decision as to what it finally becomes! *This* is a gigantic lesson for every Christian to learn. There is a principle in our textbook that our tree instructor would like for us to comprehend in Romans 8:28. Pay close attention to the latter part of the scripture.

And we know that all things work together for good to them that love God, to them who are the called according to his purpose

Did we catch the last part of the scripture? As God's children, the tree would like for us to come to grips with the solemn fact that we are called "according to *His* purpose," not ours. Just like the tree, it is our responsibility to grow as best we can, under the watchful and conscientious eye of our Divine Caretaker and in *His* time, we will become whatever it is that He, in His infinite wisdom, has cultivated us to be. Some trees become crosses. Some trees become the inner workings of houses. Some trees become furniture. There is an endless array of things that require the services of a tree! However, some trees never "travel." Their purpose is to stay right where they are– to produce fruit that feeds people everywhere. Hear this! Some trees do not even produce fruit! They are in place for one moment in time–to stop an arrow, deflect a bullet, or provide a place of hiding for a legitimate fugitive. One moment in time! And once that purpose is served, they just continue to stand, content to have been called upon to serve their Master, their Creator. This, dear student, is the initial lesson our wooden professor would have us learn. This same principle is articulated in 1 Corinthians 12:11 which pleads with us to grasp the principle that the Holy Spirit distributes the gifts of the Spirit as He sees fit. *We* do not get to choose or demand. It is up to the Holy Spirit. This does not mean we cannot pray for specific gifts; it just means we must pattern our prayers after our Master in the garden when He prayed "nevertheless not as I will, but as Thou wilt"(Matthew 26:39).

To walk in perfect trust and dependence upon our Heavenly Father, we must truly embrace this all-important principle. In I Corinthians 12:11we are told, *"But all these worketh that one and the selfsame Spirit, dividing to every man severally as he will."*The Holy Spirit divides the gifts as *He* sees it or as *He wills*. 1 Timothy 6:6 reminds us that *"Godliness with contentment is great gain."* We also learn the object lesson of contentment from the tree. Whether it is being an intricate part of some grand architectural masterpiece or providing the wood for a toothpick – the tree is just content to be used by the Master in whatever capacity the Creator deems appropriate.

Positioning is the next lesson that we learn from our teacher the tree. At the very inception of its life it begins to position itself, to establish itself, to prepare itself to stand and withstand when the various trials and tribulations of life are hurled in its direction. For a variety of reasons, a tree is only as strong as its root system. Our tree teacher would have us refer to our textbook at this time. We will prayerfully consider Psalms 11:3. It provides for us the following insight: *"If the foundations be destroyed, what can the righteous do?"*

This is a powerful principle! Did you catch it? If it doesn't start right, there is not much that can be done afterward without tearing up the entire foundation! If the root system of the tree is not what it should be, it will not be able to gather the nutrients it needs to survive. If by some miracle it did grow anyway, the first strong gust of wind or the first tree that fell against it, or the first car that crashed into it would knock it down. But if the roots are right, if they go deep into the earth, seeking and searching for life-giving water, seeking the nutrients in the soil that will be exactly what that unique and specific tree needs; the tree will survive internally. Those same deep roots that provide internal strength, at the very same time provide external strength as well! When strong winds blow the tree is not moved because its roots run deep. If things run into the tree, the things and not the tree sustain the brunt of the damage.

Are you writing these things down in the notebook of your heart? Our heaven-sent instructor is striving to educate us on a matter that is extremely vital to our Christian growth and development. If we are not growing on the inside, deep within ourselves where no one else can see, if we are not allowing the Holy Spirit to have His way with the things that relate to our character, our ways, our manner of thinking, our responses and reactions to adverse situations, then in the trial, it is impossible for us to stand or withstand. We will fail, because we are not rooted and grounded on the inside. Listen to how our textbook says it in Colossians 2:7

"Rooted and built up in him, and stablished in the faith, as ye have been taught, abounding therein with thanksgiving."

In this scripture we see the Divine order of all things that God has created. We go down before we go up. We must be rooted before we can be built up or else there will be nothing to sustain what is built. God's principles and object lessons *always* make sense. They are reasonable.

I hope you are catching the additional principle of patience that accompanies this lesson as well.

It requires patience and faith to wait on our root systems to fully develop. That is why we must continually keep our eyes on our Master, for He will tell us when it is time to do what.

The final lesson that the tree will give us at this time is the lesson of unquestioning obedience. This lesson is taught by many, many instructors in God's educational institution of Nature. What is unquestioning obedience? It is exactly what it says. It is obedience without asking one single question. It is obedience without the slightest hesitancy. It is obedience that "moves as it wonders." Did you catch that last phrase? There is nothing wrong with wondering why in the world God would have you do *this* right now if you are moving or doing what He has asked you to do while you are wondering.

This lesson is vividly brought out by the tree as it relates to when it buds. There is a Divine time clock that is placed deep within the heart of every created thing. It tells the bear when to hibernate and when to wake up. It tells the geese when to migrate South. It tells the squirrel when to stop burying nuts. It is a part of the Creator's masterpiece – His timing that He has placed within His creation. The tree operates on timing, but it also operates on what we will call "environmental indicators." What am I saying? God has placed within the tree and the flower an obedience that often is an obedience unto the death. It is programmed into the tree that after a prolonged and extended winter, when the weather reaches a certain temperature for a certain length of time, to bud. No questions asked. It *obeys*! It doesn't matter that a big frost is going to come afterward and destroy most, if not all, of its buds. It does what it has been programmed to do!

Did you hear that? Did you catch that? Did you write that in the notebook of your heart?

Sometimes God will ask us to do something that will cost us all or almost everything! If we are positive that God has said it, we are not to question, we are not to hesitate–not even for a moment! This is the lesson of unquestioning obedience that we learn from the tree. This is the way of the Saviour. He must have unquestioning obedience because this means our faith in Him is strong. Hebrews 11:6 admonishes us that we cannot please God if we do not have faith, and we cannot have faith if we will obey only when it makes sense to us. There is a chorus in a Christian song that states "God is too wise to be mistaken. God is too good to be unkind. So, when you don't understand, and you can't see His hand, when you can't trace His hand, trust His heart." The tree trusts completely in the heart of its Creator. It is that trust, that faith alone, that empowers it to act unquestioningly. We must ask the Lord in prayer to show us how to cultivate that level of "tree-like trust" so we too, can bud and blossom whenever He tells us too. Unquestioning faith and trust in His timing, in the purpose He has for us, in His foundation building principles for us – this is His way, His will, and this is because He loves us and knows what is best. Will you continue to learn of Him?

Lessons from the Tree:

- We cannot limit God as to how He will use us.
- As God's children, we are on earth for God's purpose, not our own.
- We do not determine what gifts or talents we will possess. That is up to the Holy Spirit.
- The tree teaches us to be content with what God has called you to be or to do.

- Much in life depends on how we position or prepare ourselves to meet the difficulty.
- A tree is only as strong as its root system.
- If the foundation is not right, there is not much that can be done without tearing up the faulty foundation and starting over.
- If we do not allow God to fortify us on the inside, in our character, we will fail when faced with adversity.
- In God's divine order, we must go down before we go up to be truly successful.
- It requires patience to wait on our root systems to grow correctly.
- Christians must allow God to cultivate in them unquestioning obedience.
- It is acceptable to "wonder while you are moving".

The Bird

God placed within me something special. He gave me a wondrous gift.

Naturally, without trying, I myself, can rise and lift

From off this earth into the heavens, I myself can soar and fly!

And I never stop and question, I don't ask My Creator why

I defy the laws of gravity, I cannot be bound to land.

Man tries his best to imitate me, but he can't truly understand.

Hummingbirds go forth or backwards, up or down, from side to side.

Majestic eagles catch the airways and effortlessly upon them glide.

I build my nests how God instructs me, I do exactly as I am told.

I don't know where My next meal comes from.
I just let each day unfold.

I trust implicitly in My Creator, this makes my life anxiety-free.

I somehow know what ere the trial – God will indeed take care of me.

I sing my song of praise God gave me. Nothing can prevent my voice

From extolling always my Creator, it's in my nature to rejoice!

To man my mindset is unbelievable, it borders on insane, absurd,

But I am what the Creator made me, I sing and fly because I am a bird.

Derek Arthur Sharpe

The Bird

F rom the soaring majesty of the eagle to the amazing wonderment of the hummingbird, each one of these winged masterpieces of the Creator offer Divine lessons that have been implanted by the Sovereign of the universe into their very being. We enter now into the classroom of the bird. We will have various instructors, but be assured, each one of them has been thoroughly prepared and is divinely accredited to teach the principles of its Maker to all who would have an ear to hear.

All we must do is live near trees to understand this first lesson of Heaven from our winged instructors. We will sit at the feet of the cardinal, the robin, the sparrow, and the finch as they collectively teach the following principle of Heaven: In sunshine, in rain, in feast, and in famine- sing. It is important to understand that when birds sing they are praising God! If you have ever been privileged to hear the birds sing in the early morning hours, you *know* that they are praising their Creator. They have been "programmed for praise," and their symphony of adoration resounds throughout the forests, the dales, the meadows, and even throughout the neighborhoods where there are trees and shrubbery that will house them.

Take special note of the principle. It matters not how much food they caught or found the previous day, they awaken with praise and adoration in their very beings and burst forth in sweet melodies of gratitude and appreciation for another day! God IS a provider. This is the secret that all creation knows so well. He *can* and *will* take care of every need. The principle of praise that the birds know so well is captured in two important passages in our textbook. We will consider one from the Old Testament and another from the New. We will be going to Psalms 34:1 and 1 Thessalonians 5:18. Hear what the Lord Himself has to say about praise. Psalm 34:1 reads:

"I will bless the Lord at all times: his praise shall continually be in my mouth."

And from the New Testament 1 Thessalonians 5:18 informs us:

"*In everything give thanks: for this is the will of God in Christ Jesus concerning you.*"

Did you notice the common thread of instruction that ran through both verses? Not just praise, *continual* praise, never ending praise, *always* praise! This is the lesson that is taught so well by our tiny, melodious instructors. Circumstances do not dictate their praise. Rain cannot prevent them from praising God. Even in relentless heat and bitter cold, we can hear them doing what they love to do, praising their Creator!

Our flying teachers point us to a critical message in 1 Thessalonians 5:18. We must take note of what the verse does not say, what it does not require. They would have you embrace what it *did not say*, what it *did not require*. The verse *does not* tell us to give thanks to God *for* everything; it tells us to give thanks to God *in* everything. There is a *huge* difference. The difference between a loving, caring, reasonable Heavenly Father and an unfeeling, controlling, dictator. Our loving Saviour does not require us to praise Him *for* tragedy. When parents have lost their eight-year-old son in a car accident, the Lord does not require that they praise Him for their precious little boy being killed. That would be cruel. What He *does* require is a faith that *knows*, according to 1 Corinthians 10:13, He would not allow it, if they could not bear it. So, *during our sorrow*, just like our feathery instructors have modeled for us, we are to find something for which to praise God. The wonderful thing is praise lightens the load and gives us the strength to bear the burden of the adversity. Praise is a tremendous weapon and we must truly digest this critical life lesson from our instructors who have been gifted with the ability to fly. No matter what or where, praise is the answer.

The next lesson we will learn from our winged instructors is found within the nests that they build. The architectural ingenuity that goes into the nests built by birds is amazing! Pay close attention to a small sampling of the types of nests that birds construct.

"The cup nest is smoothly hemispherical inside, with a deep depression to house the eggs. Most are made of pliable materials—including grasses—though a small number are made of mud or saliva. Many passerines and a few non-passerines, including some hummingbirds and some swifts, build this type of nest.

Many raptors, like the Osprey, use the same huge platform nest for years, adding new material each season. Some water birds, including the grebes, build floating platform nests. The platform nest is a large structure, often many times the size of the (typically large) bird which has built it. Depending on the species, these nests can be on the ground or elevated. In the case of raptor nests, or eyries (also spelt aerie), these are often used for many years, with new material added each breeding season. In some cases, the nests grow large enough to cause structural damage to the tree itself, particularly during bad storms where the weight of the nest can cause additional stress on wind-tossed branches.

The pendant nest is an elongated sac woven of pliable materials such as grasses and plant fibers and suspended from a branch. Oropendolas, caciques, orioles, weavers and sunbirds are among the species that weave pendant nests. The sphere nest is a roundish structure; it is completely enclosed, except for a small opening which allows access."(8)

There is no class required to attend, no school for certification, no years and years of toiling, striving to make the grade so they can one day be authorized to build and construct. Birds just do it! Birds do not take into consideration the difficulty of the task. They just start the project and finish the project. What is the lesson? What GOD has called you to do does not require the approval of man. If *He* has placed it within you to do it *and* has told you to do it *now*, then it matters not what anyone else says. Do what the Lord has called you to do. There will always be doubters who will tell you that you will *never* be able to achieve that which God has told you to pursue. Listen to *God* and pursue your God-given destiny anyway!

Birds do not take into consideration the difficulty of the task. They *just start the project* and *finish the project*! This is the very important lesson to be learned. Furthermore, if God has told you to do it, then He has already placed within you the ability to do it. One inspired writer comments: "As the will of man co-operates with the will of God, it becomes omnipotent. Whatever is to be done at His command may be accomplished in His strength. All His biddings are enabling."(9) It may require schooling at an inconvenient season of your life. It may require you attempting to do something that *you* do not even believe you have the capacity and ability to perform, but if God has told you to do it, you must do just as the bird instructors above, just begin. Consider this principle from Luke 17:12-14:

12 And as he entered into a certain village, there met him ten men that were lepers, which stood afar off:

13 And they lifted up their voices, and said, Jesus, Master, have mercy on us.

14 And when he saw them, he said unto them, Go shew yourselves unto the priests. And it came to pass, that, as they went, they were cleansed"

Did you catch the principle? They asked Jesus for healing. They *wanted* to be healed. Jesus did not heal them right there on the spot. He told them to go to the priest and have the priest pronounce that they were no longer lepers! But they *were still* lepers! The Bible says *as they went*, they were cleansed.

Sometimes we will not see the way clear that Jesus has instructed until we by faith, begin the journey. This is the lesson we glean from our Heaven appointed flying instructors.

Whatever God has placed within you to do, just do it. God will take care of the rest.

Our final lesson is from the eagle. The king of all birds, the sovereign of all flying fowl. His lesson is one that has been taught over and over, but it must be included in *this course*. In short, the eagle teaches us to use adversity to propel us higher. When the problems come our way, we must allow God to show us how to make the problem catapult us to success. This is the lesson of our eagle instructor! It behooves us to pay prayerful attention to what one inspired writer shares about the ability of the eagle. Pay prayerful attention. It is a life molding moment.

"However, as I researched more, I found out a little bit about the flying patterns of these majestic birds. While they may not fly above storms, they are quite adept at using strong winds to their advantage.

Eagles do use the winds (and some quite strong), as well as "updrafts" coming off hills and mountains. This helps them to gain altitude and set them up for a long, soaring flight to another location. They may not fly above the storms, but they are able to use the strength of the storm to propel them in their journey. And perhaps, that's why God says that those who trust in Him will "soar on wings like eagles" (Isaiah 40:28-31).

He doesn't promise that we won't have to face the storms, but that as we seek Him and His glory, He will use trials to bring about good (Romans 8:28). He says He provides strength to those who are tired, not that the tired will not have to keep on walking. Just like you have to journey through some valleys in order to stand on the mountaintops, so the proper confidence in God can use the stormy winds of life to bring you to the place that He wants you to be, allowing you to sail higher – i.e. glorifying Him more - than you ever would have without those storms.

We may not be able to avoid the storms. In fact, as Christians, God promises that we will experience them (John 16:33). But that doesn't mean we can't soar. It doesn't mean that we won't get to where God desires us to be. In fact, it may be the storm that brings us there."(10)

Absolutely outstanding!

What a powerful lesson from the king of all flying fowl. I pray you have learned well the lessons of the birds. They, too, have shown us the way of our Creator, His will, and His love. May we hold these precious lessons close to our hearts and never let them go.

Lessons from the Bird:

- In all circumstances, no matter what, sing. Find something for which to praise God.
- All creation operates under the principle that God is the provider. He takes care of every need.
- We are required to praise God *in* everything, not *for* everything.
- Even amid sorrow, there is something for which we can praise the Lord.
- Praise lightens the load and allows us to bear the burden of the adversity.
- Praise is a weapon in Spiritual warfare.
- What God has called someone to do does not require the approval of man.
- Birds do not take into consideration the difficulty of the task. They just begin the task and complete the task because of their reliance upon God.
- Sometimes, we will not see our way clear until after we have begun to do what God instructed.
- We must use adversity to propel us higher.
- Often it is the storms in our lives that take us to higher heights

The Coney

The Bible says the Coney is quite feeble, weak, not strong.
And since it is defenseless, it knows where it belongs.
He makes his house within the rocks, in there he's safe from harm.
It gives protection from all danger, in winter it keeps him warm.
Although he's weak, the Scripture calls the Coney exceeding wise,
It's that he knows that he's not strong, therein his wisdom lies.
He's knows security is in the rock, in there he is protected.
It's when he ventures forth from there, that's when he is subjected
To all that would destroy him, to sorrows and to woes.
And so, he does not go too far, from the safety that he knows.
When out he must be ever watchful, always on alert
For any sound or indication that this could cause him hurt.
He can't become absorbed, consumed, he must avoid distraction,
At any moment they could become his last fatal attraction.
The Lord would have us all to learn from our furry little friend,
Our only protection is in Christ, He will keep us until the end.

Derek Arthur Sharpe

The Coney

O ur final instructor in our Nature curriculum is a tiny, defenseless, furry little creature that has a much-elevated status as a Divine instructor, for it is named in our textbook as one of the educators whose course we must take. I introduce you to the Coney. We will begin with the endorsement of the Master of all creation, so all will have a sense of confidence, taking a class from so unassuming and seemingly insignificant a teacher as the Coney. Pay attention to the Divine recommendation found in Proverbs 30:24-28.

> *24 There be four things which are little upon the earth, but they are exceeding wise:*
> *25 The ants are a people not strong, yet they prepare their meat in the summer;*

26 The conies are but a feeble folk, yet make they their houses in the rocks;

27 The locusts have no king, yet go they forth all of them by bands;

28 The spider taketh hold with her hands and is in kings' palaces.

Now, we are commanded to "get wisdom" (Proverbs 4:7) and whenever God Himself tells us that something is "exceeding wise," we need to take out our pad and pen and begin to take notes. What are the lessons to be gleaned from our furry little instructor?

The Bible confirms that the Coney is feeble, weak, and defenseless. What then, is his answer to his condition or shortcomings? *He makes his house in the rocks!* Because the Coney *knows and acknowledges his weakness,* he *dwells—spends much of his time in, abides in*–the shelter of the rock. Oh, if every Christian could take this class that you are taking right now! Our textbook tells us that we can't do *anything* without Christ.(John 15:5) It also tells us what the Coney knows, that Christ is *the Rock*! Let us go in our textbooks to 1 Corinthians 10:4 and truly listen to what it says:

"And did all drink the same spiritual drink: for they drank of that spiritual Rock that followed them: and that Rock was Christ."

Jesus is the Rock! He is our shelter and just like our Coney instructor, we are to stay under the shelter of His protection! *This* is what makes the Coney so wise! He knows he has absolutely no protection or defense against all the various predators that are seeking to devour him. His only safety lies in staying close to the rock. Did you catch that lesson? He never wanders so far away from the safety of the rock that he cannot get to it *quickly* in an emergency.

The Bible teaches us in Proverbs 18:10 that *"The name of the Lord is a strong tower: the righteous runneth into it and is safe."* What is the "Name of the Lord'? It is in this wonderful Name that our Coney instructor counsels us to find protection. In Exodus 33 God and Moses are having a conversation. God tells Moses that He knows Moses perfectly inside and out. Moses then makes an unbelievable request of God. He asked God to allow him to know God the way God knows him! Amazing! Let us see exactly how Moses worded this question. Prayerfully consider the wording of Moses' request in Exodus 33:13. *Now therefore, I pray thee, if I have found grace in thy sight, shew me now thy way, that I may know thee, that I may find grace in thy sight: and consider that this nation is thy people.*

Now, consider verses 17 and 18 of the same chapter in which Moses made the same request, but with different wording.

> *17 And the Lord said unto Moses, I will do this thing also that thou hast spoken: for thou hast found grace in my sight, and I know thee by name.*
> *18 And he said, I beseech thee, shew me thy glory.*

We cannot miss this. God said, "I know thee *by name*." Moses' reply was "*Shew me thy way*" and then he reiterated his petition by asking "*Shew me they glory*." In response to His telling Moses He knew him by name, Moses asked God to tell him *His* name. However, he used a different phrase so that we could understand what name means from God's perspective. Let's continue with their conversation. We pick it up in verse 19, the very next verse.

> *And he said, I will make all my goodness pass before thee, and I will proclaim the name of the Lord before*

thee; and will be gracious to whom I will be gracious, and will shew mercy on whom I will shew mercy"

Moses, in response to God telling him he knew Moses by name, asked God to show him His way and His glory. God's response to Moses' request was I will proclaim the Name of the Lord. It gets clearer. Exodus 34:5-7 is where we find God's answer to Moses' request:

5 And the Lord descended in the cloud, and stood with him there, and proclaimed the name of the Lord. 6 And the Lord passed by before him, and proclaimed, The Lord, The Lord God, merciful and gracious, longsuffering, and abundant in goodness and truth, 7 Keeping mercy for thousands, forgiving iniquity and transgression and sin, and that will by no means clear the guilty; visiting the iniquity of the fathers upon the children, and upon the children's children, unto the third and to the fourth generation.

The Name of the Lord that He proclaimed was His characteristics. The Name of the Lord, the Way of the Lord, and the Glory of the Lord, is the *character of God!*

It is becoming clear what the Coney is striving to teach us. The Name of the Lord or the Character of God is the strong tower; it is the rock that keeps us safe from the enticements of the enemy. It is God's character that is a refuge in time of trouble. It is as we surrender our will to His will, our nature to His nature, our weak and wavering characteristics for His strong and steadfast characteristics, that we, in our weakness become strong (2 Corinthians 12:9) The Rock is Christ. His character is our shelter and defense. It is the exceeding wisdom of the Coney that instructs us to stay, to dwell, to abide in the character of Jesus. What a precious lesson!

There is another lesson we can learn from our weak and feeble teacher. It is the lesson of unnecessary exposure. The Coney realizes that there are times that he must leave the rock. Food is outside of the rock. Water is outside of the rock. Conies live mainly off grass. A single Coney can gather as much as a bushel of hay in preparation for the winter. They don't go out for anything other than the gathering of food and water. The Coney doesn't get cabin fever and just "have to get out for a while."

Sometimes we as Christians, "get tired" of doing the right thing and "just want to have some fun" for a minute. It is at these critical moments that we needlessly expose ourselves to the wily temptations of our great adversary the devil who is always walking about as a lion, seeking whom he may devour (1 Peter 5:8). The lesson of unnecessary exposure is a critical one for every Christian to learn from our Divinely appointed Coney instructor.

The final lesson that we will learn from the Coney is that he delights to stay in the rock. The reason why the Coney gathers so much grass or hay, even as much as a bushel per Coney, is because the Coney does not hibernate. He does not sleep during the long winter. He is wide awake the entire time. He is delighted and content to stay in that rock all winter long, delighted to stay in a place of safety all winter long, delighted to stay where it is warm and cozy all winter long. This is the mindset that we must learn from the Coney. We cannot get "restless" in Jesus. David said, "I delight to do Thy will O my God, yea, Thy law is within my heart." (Psalms 40:8)

This is the secret of the Coney. God Himself placed the desire within the Coney to stay in the rock during the winter. God Himself placed within the Coney the drive to avoid exposing itself unnecessarily to danger. It is not something the Coney has to think about; it's in his heart. David tells us that the way that we can delight in the Lord is to allow the

Lord to place His law in our hearts just as He did the Coney. God is more than able and more than willing to begin the process right here and right now.

As we end our session on object lessons from the educational institution of Nature, let us fervently pray that we will implement, by the grace of God and in His strength, each one of the lessons we have been exposed to, that we may indeed be successful in learning of Christ, His way, His will, His love.

Lessons from the Coney:

- It is wise to know and acknowledge our weakness.
- As Christians we are never to depend upon ourselves, but always depend upon Christ.
- The Way of the Lord and the Glory of the Lord are interchangeable.
- God's Way and God's Glory represent God's character.
- The characteristics of God offer security and safety against the weapons of the world.
- It is never wise to unnecessarily expose ourselves to the enticements of the enemy.

- Christian maturity brings a satisfaction with the Christ like lifestyle.
- Often "one moment of fun" can have life altering/ending consequences.
- It is easy to stay in a place that you love.
- We must allow God to place His love in our heart which enables us to love to be in His presence and to stay in His presence.
- When there is no delight, discontentment will eventually manifest itself.
- Small things can teach big lessons.

We have received excellent insight from our instructors in nature. God will now have us transition to another institution of learning. It is quite possibly the broadest, deepest, most expansive of all God's educational institutions. It is the educational institution of Life. Although it may appear somewhat overwhelming, it is nonetheless a true statement that God Himself has ordained that life itself and all that it encompasses is supposed to be educational. Consider prayerfully what God declares in Deuteronomy 6:6- 9 as it relates to the parameters of a God-ordained educational curriculum.

6 And these words, which I command thee this day, shall be in thine heart:

7 And thou shalt teach them diligently unto thy children, and shalt talk of them when thou sittest in thine house, and when thou walkest by the way, and when thou liest down, and when thou risest up.

8 And thou shalt bind them for a sign upon thine hand, and they shall be as frontlets between thine eyes.

9 And thou shalt write them upon the posts of thy house, and on thy gates.

No Summer break for those who attend God's school! No eight o'clock to four o'clock for those who are enrolled in Heaven's educational institute of higher learning. God declares that diligent instruction takes place when we are sitting in the house, when we are walking by the way, when we are about to go to bed and when we are waking up in the morning. In short, *all day, wherever we are, no matter what we are doing-learning is taking place!* The scripture goes on to break down to us that there should be something on our hands that reminds us that we are in school. It also declares that things should be put up all around us that reinforce the educational lessons that have been and are being taught! *Life is indeed one gigantic schoolroom.*

Unfortunately, ever since sin entered the earth, Satan has an institution of learning as well. The lessons we learn from life have everything to do with *who* serves as instructor. Therefore Matthew 11:28-30 is constantly being reviewed and reiterated in almost every class you attend–"take My yoke upon you and learn of Me." There is no getting around it, we will learn *as* we live. The question each of us must constantly ask ourselves is am I learning the things of God or the things of Satan? Is what I am exposing myself to teaching me the characteristics of the Creator of heaven and earth or am I being exposed to the characteristics of the thief who can *only* kill, steal, and destroy? At every step of our educational journey Satan will be striving to induce us to "transfer" to his school. He declares that the tuition cost is lower, the classes are easier, and the degrees are distributed in much less time. We must not be seduced by his lies. God's school gives life and life more abundantly. You have made the decision to learn of Christ–His will, His way, and His love.

Students, God's class, is now in session.

Time

It's something that you cannot see, or smell, or hear, or feel,

But abstract as it may appear, it is indeed quite real.

It impacts your entire life, in fact, it's the foundation.

How each respond to it, quite frankly, determines one's salvation.

At birth we each receive our part, our Divine allocation.

The impact of decisions made are beyond man's calculation.

It is a talent from the Lord, you could call it a gift.

This precious trust, the evil one is constantly seeking to sift.

The gift of time, this gift from God, must be earnestly cultivated.

But most within our busy world are hardly motivated

To fight the battle to master time, to not even waste an hour.

We'd be surprised how much would change,
that it would give us power

To accomplish things that hitherto were far beyond our reach.

To be more aware of every minute, is the sermon we should preach.

So, couched within the confines of this short and concise rhyme

Is the sacred scriptural principle – we must redeem the time.

Derek Arthur Sharpe

Time

Your first life instructor is Professor Time. He is some-times referred to as Father Time because he has been teaching so long. His class is one of the most difficult for students to pass, but he is as patient as he is wise and if you are faithful and pay attention, you will do just fine. The very first lesson that time must teach is the far-reaching results of wasting time. Time literally is a part of every second of life. If we are alive and in our right mind, then God holds us accountable for what we do with our time, which, is *His* time. That's right-we do not have any time of our own. It is all God's time and we are assessed on how well we put *His* time to use. Professor Time wants to instill within us the principle that time is a talent or a gift from God and how we use, misuse, or waste this talent has a direct bearing not only on the grade we receive for his class, but more importantly, it often has a direct impact upon our salvation. Time is a part of everything we do. Consider what Ecclesiastes 3:1 tells us regarding time: *"To everything there is a season, and a time to every purpose under the heaven."*

The Bible teaches us that there is a time, a season, to everything. The next seven verses of Ecclesiastes 3 continue a long list of examples as it relates to time: A time to dance and a time to weep. A time to build and a time to tear down. A time to hate and a time to love. A time for peace and a time for war. A time to live and a time to die. And so on, to name a few.

The critical lesson Professor Time strives to teach us at the very onset of this course is that *timing is everything.* *When* we do what we do is often more important than *what* we do! For example, if I know that a person is getting ready to step into a hole that is ten feet in front of them, it would be kind of me to inform them that there is a hole *before* they reach the hole.

However, it would be unkind of me to inform the person *after* he or she has stepped into the hole or with insufficient time to avoid the hole. Although the information was the same, *when* the information was given was critical. Timing is everything.

The Instructor is about to share an uncomfortable truth with us and at this point in the class it is usually his custom to allow the students to mentally brace themselves for what he is about to share.

Prepare to hear some insight that is going to change our lives for the better, but possibly make us somewhat uncomfortable in the process. Here it is. How we deal with time is a direct reflection on our character, the only thing that God judges us on. You heard it right. God will not judge us on whether we have a college degree or a master's or even a doctorate, but he *will* judge us on how we spent the time He lent us. God will not judge us on whether we became rich and famous. Nor will He judge us on the size of our houses or cars, but He WILL judge us on the choices we make regarding His time. Put another way, we are all stewards of God's time. He has placed us on this earth to use *His* time to further *His* plan and the extent to which we do or do not do that-literally will determine our destiny. Time, our time, God's time, the gift of time, how to use time, should be of vital importance to all who want to learn of Christ. Time and timing have everything to do with His will, His way, and His love. 2 Peter 2:9 tells us that it is not God's will that any should perish. Therefore, in His mercy He gives individuals time after time to come to Him. The characteristics of longsuffering and kindness, patience and forbearance have everything to do with time. It is the very nature of God to give you enough time to be saved. No matter how long it takes, no matter what it takes, if God knows that a person will eventually truly and sincerely come to Him, God will give that individual time. God would indeed be an unjust and unfair God if He knew that in 50 years a person would genuinely repent of all their wicked ways and become a true follower of God and then allow Satan to take that person's life at the thirty-year point. Praise God that NEVER happens! And since that is an attribute or characteristic of God, He expects us to allow His Holy Spirit to download that exact same mindset into us, so we too can display that kind of patient forbearance towards those who are being particularly difficult to deal with. It is not only His will but His way to be longsuffering and kind to the wayward and the wicked, the mean and the stubborn, the rebellious and the ungrateful. Why? Because of His great love! Time truly teaches us that to learn of Christ, we must appreciate the value of time. Time and salvation go hand in hand.

Professor Time would also like to make us aware of an insidious enemy of time. Some accurately refer to it as the "thief of time."

We will now be introduced to one of Satan's most accomplished devices to rob people of their time, their character, and ultimately their salvation–procrastination, the enemy of time. Satan knows that God operates on certain principles. One of those principles is the dynamic of "probation." Probation has everything to do with time. In the spiritual language of the Bible, "daytime" represents the period when individuals are still able to surrender their lives to Christ no matter how horrible they have been or what vile and wicked things they have done. Probation gives us time to repent and come to Jesus and be forgiven and cleansed from all we have done.(1 John 1:9) Of course, if daytime represents probation being open or available, then 'nighttime' or darkness represents the period when probation has closed, and salvation is no longer available.

Let us consider the story of "Noah and the Ark." It is a painfully accurate depiction of the misuse of time and the concept of probation. Genesis 7:16 states that the Lord "shut him in." Three simple words with gigantic significance in their solemn awfulness. If the door to the ark was open, any and everyone was free to get on the ark and be saved from the devastating impact of the flood, but as soon as God "shut the door", probation had closed, time had run out, and salvation was no longer available to the inhabitants of the earth. A vast number of people did not take advantage of the time granted to them and lost not only their lives, but eternal life because they did not use their time wisely. Listen attentively to See the principle articulated in John 9:4.

I must work the works of him that sent me, while it is day: the night cometh, when no man can work.

The Bible teaches that if it is day (not a literal daylight, but a spiritual time where the heart is still open to light), Jesus is still able to access the heart and change it for good. But once the night comes, which represents the heart becoming so cold, dark, and hard that it refuses to allow Jesus to come in and help, probation closes, Satan wins, and that poor unfortunate soul is forever lost. We must pay close attention to this important lesson.

This fateful condition of condemnation and despair began with procrastination. There was a point in their lives when the individuals heard the sweet, still small voice of

Christ beckoning them to Him. They did not resist, they just chose to do it later. This is a poor use of time.

That which you are to do, do not delay; do it now!

The habit of doing what we are supposed to do when we are supposed to do it, is the greatest habit we can cultivate as it relates to time. The Bible declares that many will be lost because they knew not the time of their visitation. (Luke 19:44)

Dear students, Professor Time pleads with you to learn this oh so valuable lesson. Begin now to cultivate the habit of using time wisely. Your salvation could very well depend on it. Professor Time usually ends with the following scripture found in Romans 13:11, 12. Keep it close to your heart as you attend the remainder of the classes. Prayerfully consider what it says and never forget its message:

11 And that, knowing the time, that now it is high time to awake out of sleep: for now is our salvation nearer than when we believed.

12 The night is far spent; the day is at hand: let us therefore cast off the works of darkness and let us put on the armour of light.

Did you catch it? Time has much to do with our salvation! And it is high time that we cast off the works of procrastination and put on the armor of Spirit-led time management. The correct use of time protects us from much of the evil that Satan will send our way! The Instructor of Time has completed this section of his class. You will see him again in Time 102 and Time 103, for there is much, much more to learn as it relates to time and its value. As you learn of time as God views time, you will indeed be learning of His will, His way, and His love.

Lessons from time:

- Wasting time has far-reaching results.
- God holds us accountable for what we do with our time, which is actually His time.
- Time is a gift or talent from God to us.
- How we use, or misuse time can have a direct impact upon our salvation.
- There is a time or a season for everything.
- Often *when* something is said or done, is more important than *what* is said or done.
- Timing is everything.

- God has made each of us stewards of *His* time.

- How we deal with time is a direct reflection of our character.

- God is not as concerned with our accomplishments as He is with how well we used our time.

- God will wait even if it takes years for a person to truly come to Him.

- We must allow God to cultivate His patience and longsuffering into our lives that we may display His character to others who are unkind and unlikable.

- Time and salvation go hand in hand.

- Procrastination is an insidious enemy of time.

- It is not a wise use of time to put off for tomorrow what can be done today.

- The correct use of time protects us from much of the evil Satan would send our way.

Influence

There is something that surrounds us, it's everywhere we go.

It is a literal atmosphere, an environment that's high or low.

It permeates our very being, it's contagious to the touch.

Often unconscious, but still quite potent, it determines oh so much.

It has turned the tide of battles, it has altered great elections.

It has had a significant role within most of life's major selections.

It too is a precious talent, from God a sacred trust,

To become aware of this great gift, indeed is an absolute must.

Like a pebble thrown into a lake, the waves widen to the shore,

So, our influence has the exact effect and often so much more.

It is only in eternity that we can truly ever know,

The extent of our influence, just how far it did go.

Heavy with the chill of gloom or bearing the fragrance of love,

Our influence comes from down beneath or is unctioned from above.

Conscious or unconsciously we impact those within our sphere,

So, let's be more conscientious of all we do while we are here.

Derek Arthur Sharpe

Influence

Your next instructor has almost the same impeccable credentials as Professor Time. She has been on every continent in the world! She has experience with the most elite and wealthiest individuals on the planet; at the same time, she has spent an equal amount of time amidst the lowliest, the most wicked and depraved, poverty-stricken and forsaken class of people! High or low, rich or poor, intelligent or ignorant, honest or dishonest, righteous or wicked, she has vast and extensive experience with them all! Her classes have been held everywhere that people exist. She has a reputation of being very easy to get along with, but her coursework is demanding and somewhat overwhelming.

Class, I now introduce Professor Influence.

Professor Influence has an intimate knowledge of the Creator of the universe and as such, she is more than qualified to instruct us on the profound relationship between influence and His way, His will, and His love. It is customary for the class to come to the uncomfortable realization at the very onset of this course that influence is something that every one of us exerts *and are held accountable for by God*. She is fond of telling students to think of influence as impact and to think of impact as a blow. Literally, each person who enters our presence is hit, impacted, influenced by something about us and this happens whether we try to do it or not. Our influence shapes and molds what others think of us, how others view us. This in turn, has much to do with whether they respect or disrespect us, listen to us or disregard us. The gift of influence, as stated earlier, is not just for the rich and famous. Everyone has been given the gift, the talent of influence, and God expects us to cultivate it to His honor and glory. Influence is very closely connected to reputation.

The story of Daniel is a wonderful depiction of the powerful impact that a person's influence and reputation can have on everyone –those who are for us and those who are against us. Daniel's life captures the importance of (1) Choosing to make the right decision before we are faced with the decision.(Daniel 1:8) (2) Making it a habit to do the right thing over and over, consistently, thus making it custom or unconscious routine (Daniel 6:10); and finally (3) Not allowing inconvenience or adverse circumstances or consequences to sway us or derail our convictions (Daniel 6:10). Although there are many other attributes and dynamics in the life of Daniel, these three core concepts allow us to see clearly the direct correlation between the principles and a person's influence, impact, and reputation. Before continuing, Instructor Influence usually introduces the class to an old song or hymn that is not sung so much today, but indeed needs to be played, sung, and etched deep into the minds of all who are taking the classes that will enable them to learn of Christ, His will, His way, His love. The name of the song is "Dare to be a Daniel." Pay close attention to the lyrics:

Standing by a purpose true, Heeding God's command, Honor them, the faithful few! All hail to Daniel's band!

Dare to be a Daniel, Dare to stand alone! Dare to have a purpose firm! Dare to make it known.

Many mighty men are lost, Daring not to stand, Who for God had been a host By joining Daniel's band.

Many giants, great and tall, Stalking through the land, Headlong to the earth would fall, If met by Daniel's band.

Hold the Gospel banner high! On to vict'ry grand! Satan and his hosts defy, And shout for Daniel's band.

This song, written by Phillip Bliss, does much to assist Professor Influence in downloading in our minds the powerful ingredients that positively shape influence. What made Daniel who he was, and therefore what his influence, impact, or reputation was, revolved completely around his consistent resolve to stand for what he believed in.

The song declares, stand true to your purpose. Listen *only* to God's command for your life. Dare to stand even if it means you stand alone! It is this mindset that prepares us to be among the few who will be saved, as opposed to the many who will be lost. Consider prayerfully and soberly Matthew 7:13, 14:

13 Enter ye in at the strait gate: for wide is the gate, and broad is the way, that leadeth to destruction, and many there be which go in thereat:

14 Because strait is the gate, and narrow is the way, which leadeth unto life, and few there be that find it.

It is sad but true that many people today do not want the inconvenience and sometimes uncomfortable consequences of standing by their convictions. They find it much easier to "adjust" their convictions to accommodate the circumstances. Amazingly, this mindset also affects their influence and shapes and molds their reputation and impact. Those who become familiar with those "ways" conclude that the individuals can be bought, that they will not stand for what is right, if the "price is right" or the consequences are strong enough; they will fold, capitulate, give in. That, dear students, unfortunately, is the influence, the impact, the reputation of many today.

Daniel was a slave. Captured and brought to a foreign land, he was then blessed to be among a selected few who were chosen to be educated (re-educated, brainwashed) and placed in high ranking positions in this new country. Daniel consistently refused to do anything that would compromise his faith in his God and the principles and guidelines that accompanied his belief system. He quickly gained a reputation for not doing anything that was not right and just and true. That is the impact, reputation, and influence that our instructor is hoping that each one of us will strive to allow the Lord to develop in us.

If you have not learned yet, Instructor Influence must introduce you to an uncomfortable, unfortunate reality: standing for what is right will create many enemies. In Daniel's case, his sterling integrity, his unwavering purpose, his deep-seated conviction to only do that which was right, made the other powerful men in the kingdom angry. They tried everything in their power to catch Daniel doing something wrong. But they couldn't catch him doing anything wrong *because in big and small areas, Daniel did everything right.* Class, did you catch that principle? Faithfulness, carefulness, diligence in everything whether big or small, of great import or the tiniest significance, are what determine the caliber, the quality of our influence.

This determines the type of impact we have on others and therefore will determine our reputation. Read the conclusion the men who were striving to destroy Daniel had to accept. Daniel 6:4-5:

4 Then the presidents and princes sought to find occasion against Daniel concerning the kingdom; but they could find none occasion nor fault; forasmuch as he was faithful, neither was there any error or fault found in him.

5 Then said these men, We shall not find any occasion against this Daniel, except we find it against him concerning the law of his God.

That is a reputation to strive for. No error, no fault found in him. Amazing! These wicked and unsavory characters arrived at the conclusion that the only way they were going to be able to accomplish the demise or destruction of Daniel was to center it around his convictions to his God!

Professor Influence wants us to make sure we catch the implications of what was being said about Daniel's influence, impact, and reputation. It was of such sterling quality that *they couldn't even lie on Daniel because no one would believe the lie.* This is God's way. This is God's will. THIS is how God's love is displayed. Standing for what is right, cultivating an unblemished reputation, is something that we can do no matter how bad our past has been. The wonderful thing about our Lord and Saviour is that He specializes in taking individuals with horrible past reputations and empowering them to turn their lives around and develop new reputations, new impacts, and thus, a new influence.

2 Corinthians 5:17 states it this way:

Therefore, if any man be in Christ, he is a new creature: old things are passed away; behold, all things are become new.

What a tremendous concept! Old things pass away. All things become new. No more old influence! No more old impact! No more old reputation! Our Instructor can barely contain herself whenever she gets to this part of the class. It so perfectly captures the essence of *who* and *how* our Lord and Saviour is. He *can* make us new! He *can* improve our current influence or give us an entirely brand-new influence. He wants our impact to be like Daniel's. He wants our reputations to be as solid and unmovable as the tree.

Your influence is a precious gift from God. Begin in earnest today to dedicate your influence completely to Jesus because in so doing, you will be cultivating in your life His will, His way, and His love. As you pay more attention to your influence, you will be learning of Christ. You will be answering His invitation to "Learn of Me." Class dismissed. I am sure you will run into instructor Influence at various places around the campus and even after you complete your classes here. As was stated, she travels extensively, and you never can tell where you will run into her. Take a break and prepare for your next class.

Lessons from influence:

- God holds us accountable for the type of influence we exert upon others.
- Our influence shapes and molds how others perceive us.
- Influence is a gift or talent from God that must be cultivated.
- Influence is very closely connected to reputation.
- We must learn to choose to make the right decision *before* we are faced with the decision.
- Doing the right thing must become a habit, an unconscious routine.
- Inconvenience nor adversity should be able to derail a conviction.
- We must dare to stand even if it means we stand alone.

- Our convictions cannot have a price tag on them that will motivate us to abandon them.

- Standing for what is right will create many enemies.

- Faithfulness, diligence, being conscientious in the small as well as big things develops the quality of our influence.

- God can and does take those with horrible past reputations and allow them to cultivate new and powerful reputations.

Speech

There is no greater instrument for causing joy or pain.

Depending on the way it's used determines loss or gain.

The words we choose, the speech employed, reveals the inner core.

Though spoken oh so flippantly, they help us to explore

The hidden recesses in our heart, those places left untended.

Things unresolved, still open wounds, fractures yet unmended.

But words can also lift and build, they are tools of restoration.

The healing power within our words is beyond our estimation.

But speech includes not only words, we must consider our tone.

The way our words are spoken determines if God condones

The message sent, what's been conveyed, it's not just what, but how

The container of the message sounds, says reject or to allow.

Dripping with sarcasm, or permeated with true concern,

These things impact what's being said, this lesson we must learn.

Our speech is truly a talent that's been given from above

And we all must learn to cultivate it with patience, grace, and love.

Derek Arthur Sharpe

Speech

S tudents, this is one of the most significant classes in the entire "Learn of Me" Curriculum. Although each of the courses taught are of vast importance, this subject truly is the weightiest. The instructor for this course has literally been everywhere that people exist on this planet. He is fluent in every language, tongue, and dialect known to man. If it can be articulated, he can understand it. He is indeed a master teacher. I introduce you to none other than Professor Speech. Professor Speech likes to begin his class with two quotes. The first is from the greatest book in the world –the Bible.

Let us prayerfully consider Matthew 12:34-37:

34 O generation of vipers, how can ye, being evil, speak good things? for out of the abundance of the heart the mouth speaketh.

35 A good man out of the good treasure of the heart bringeth forth good things: and an evil man out of the evil treasure bringeth forth evil things.

36 But I say unto you, That every idle word that men shall speak, they shall give account thereof in the day of judgment.

37 For by thy words thou shalt be justified, and by thy words thou shalt be condemned.

This is a sobering pronouncement. It informs us that when it is all said and done, we will be graded, we will be judged, by what we say. Verse 34 introduces us to the principle that what is in our mind the most, will come out of our mouths in the form of words. Our speech is a very accurate indicator of what is going on in our minds. But we will delve deeper into this subject as the class progresses. For now, let us continue to our other introductory, ground setting quotation.

Listen attentively to this powerful principle. Professor Speech is extremely fond of this quote and always uses it to establish the foundation upon which this course is built:

The power of speech is a talent that should be diligently cultivated. Of all the gifts we have received from God, none is capable of being a greater blessing than this. With the voice we convince and persuade, with it we offer prayer and praise to God, and with it we tell others of the Redeemer's love. How important, then, that it be so trained as to be most effective for good. (11)

Professor Speech always emphasizes this statement; speech is a talent, it is a gift. As with every class that you will be taking in this eight-course section, each is, in and of itself, a gift, a talent from God!

But speech is the gift that can do the most good, that can be the greatest blessing. It must also be noted that the quote above points out that speech has power. The quote ends by stating how important it is that this power be cultivated and trained to be used for good because, if not, the power of speech will indeed be used by the great enemy of our souls. Thus, that which is capable of being the greatest blessing is also, if not surrendered completely to God, capable of being the greatest curse. Let us consider how the Bible articulates it in James 3:2-8:

2 For in many things we offend all. If any man offend not in word, the same is a perfect man, and able also to bridle the whole body.

3 Behold, we put bits in the horses' mouths, that they may obey us; and we turn about their whole body.

4 Behold also the ships, which though they be so great, and are driven of fierce winds, yet are they turned about with a very small helm, whithersoever the governor listeth.

5 Even so the tongue is a little member, and boasteth great things. Behold, how great a matter a little fire kindleth!

6 And the tongue is a fire, a world of iniquity: so is the tongue among our members, that it defileth the whole body, and setteth on fire the course of nature; and it is set on fire of hell.

7 For every kind of beasts, and of birds, and of serpents, and of things in the sea, is tamed, and hath been tamed of mankind:

8 But the tongue can no man tame; it is an unruly evil, full of deadly poison.

Class, did you grasp the tremendous power of the tongue? The Bible informs us that speech cannot be controlled by man! Only God, through the help and assistance of the Holy Spirit and a consecrated, dedicated life, can enable us to use our talent/gift of speech for good instead of evil! Verse two puts speech in proper perspective: When we allow God to completely control our speech, we are then able to allow God to completely control in every other aspect of our lives. This is the secret to a victorious life. It is through our words that we best represent the will of our Saviour, the way of our Saviour, the love of our Saviour. As we learn of Jesus, it will have an incredible impact upon the words we use, *how* we say them, *when* we say them, and *to whom* we say them. *Speech, our choice of words, is a big deal.*

The enemy of our souls came up with a catchy little phrase that those of us who are a little older were exposed to time and time again: "Sticks and stones may break my bones, but words will never harm me." For those of you who are old enough, do you remember that phrase? I am sure you do! Please pay attention to what Instructor Speech is about to share with you. *There is absolutely no truth to that statement.* As a matter of fact, the exact opposite is true! Words can be and are more harmful than physical blows! We will prayerfully consider what the greatest textbook of all time that was authored by the greatest writer of all time – The Holy Spirit, has to say. The Spirit used the wisest king to ever rule to pen the following principle found in Proverbs 18:8. Pay close attention to what it says: *The words of a talebearer are as wounds, and they go down into the innermost parts of the belly.*

Words wound. They cause pain. It is *where* they cause the pain that is so important. The Bible tells us that words bypass our physical dimension and hurt us down in our innermost belly – in our soul, the very seat of who we are! Class, this course is so important because what we say, how we say it and when we say it has an impact upon a person that impacts the very essence of an individual. There are millions of people who have been scarred for life, shaped and molded adversely, *by unkind words that have been spoken over them.*

Speech is a tremendous responsibility! No wonder we are told that we will be justified or condemned based upon our words. Our words are an accurate barometer as to the weather of our mind, the climate of our soul. The greatest advice that Professor Speech likes to share with his students is found in Colossians 4:6. When we allow the Holy Spirit to cultivate the following habits into our speech pattern, we truly become powerful instruments of righteousness, well on our way to emulating the will, the way and the love of our Master, Jesus Christ of Nazareth. Pay close attention to this speech principle, this protective barrier against allowing our words to needlessly harm another:

Let your speech be alway with grace, seasoned with salt, that ye may know how ye ought to answer every man.

This is how our Saviour allowed His words to work for Him.

Two of the biblical applications of grace are power and favor. Genesis 6:8 tells us that Noah found grace at a time when the rest of the world had fallen into disfavor with God. 2 Corinthians 12:9 tells us that God's grace is sufficient to make us strong despite our weakness and the power of Christ will attend us. So, God counsels and admonishes us through His servant Paul that our speech, our words should always be spoken with grace.

Let's break that down in these last few moments of our time together. No matter what is said, it must be said in a manner that (1) allows the person to still retain some semblance of dignity even if they are completely in the wrong and then (2) Our words should empower them to want to do better. The passage goes on to state that our words must be "seasoned with salt." Salt has two wonderful properties. It enhances and preserves what is already there. It is Christ's will, it is His way, it is His love to speak to all His children, no matter how wayward and erring, no matter how distasteful and disgusting, in this manner.

This, dear students, is what Professor Speech wants you to take from this class. For when you embrace this precious principle, you will indeed have learned of Christ. One final admonition that Instructor Speech leaves with all his students- never try to do this in your own strength. It is an exercise in frustration and discouragement because no man can tame the tongue without Jesus. Allow the Holy Spirit to empower you. There are many more classes in Speech. This was just Speech 101. Until we meet again, class dismissed.

Lessons from speech:

- All will be judged by the words that they said.
- What is in our minds the most will manifest itself in our words.
- Speech is an excellent indicator as to what is going on in the mind.
- Speech has power – for good or for evil.
- The power of speech is a talent that should be diligently cultivated.

- Speech cannot be controlled by man.

- When God has complete control of our speech, He can then control every other aspect of our lives.

- Learning of Jesus impacts the words we use, how we use them, when we use them and to whom we direct them.

- Words often can inflict more pain and damage than physical blows.

- Our words should allow a person to maintain some semblance of dignity regardless of what they have done.

- Our words should empower an individual to want to do better

- Our words should never cause a person to lose hope

Intellect

Compare it to a muscle, there must be exercise,
To never push it to its limit is not considered wise.
We each have mental capacity, it should be considered a gift.
We should be striving constantly to strengthen it and lift
It higher than it currently is, always asking for more.
Never accepting mediocrity, having excellence at the core.
The intellect is a treasure, to cherish and embrace.
It must be the priority, it must have the highest place.
The Bible tells us how we think determines who we are.
So, the caliber of information viewed must be superior by far
To the mundane and the average things this world
will strive to show us.
Treacherously they all contrive to hinder and to throw us
Into a place, an insidious mire, a dumbed down state of being,
Where we all become oblivious to what we're actually seeing.
So, guard your mind, keep it clear, make sure that it stays strong
And in God's grace and with His mind, you never will go wrong.

Derek Arthur Sharpe

Intellect

Your next instructor is a brilliant teacher. He is thoughtful, intelligent, insightful, and wise. It is impossible to learn of Christ without having taken his class. One could reasonably argue that his class is one of the most important of the entire "Learn of Me" curriculum. This class will truly require the complete and total use of all your mental faculties. Meet Instructor Intellect. Instructor Intellect goes by many names. He is referred to as mental faculties. Of course, he is also known as intelligence. Some have mistakenly referred to him as wisdom, and there are those also who believe that he is knowledge. Professor Intellect is indeed intimately connected with all these things. Anything that has to do with the function of the brain, the workings of the mind, is associated with the teacher of this course. As with the other instructors in this section, the object lessons presented deal with the proper use of the talents and gifts that have been placed at our disposal by our kind and beneficent Creator. The proper or improper use of each of the dynamics presented in this section have a critical bearing on the object lessons that are produced. It is of utmost importance that Intellect, as well as the other seven instructors in this section, make it clear to each of us that surrendering our gifts and talents to God is the only way to ensure that the object lessons that come forth from the lives of the students will be those that bring glory and honor to God and God alone. Only through the direction of the Holy Spirit will Christ's will, way, and love be portrayed. The professor of mental faculties begins each class with the foundational principle found in Proverbs 23:7

For as he thinketh in his heart, so is he: Eat and drink, saith he to thee; but his heart is not with thee.

What a principle. I am what I think! The power of the brain, the potency of our mental capacity is almost immeasurable. There is a mysterious, but very real connection between what we think and who we are. Therefore, it is important that our mind–our mindset, our intellect–is completely surrendered to God. Whoever controls the intellect controls the entire being and literally determines how the other talents and gifts are used. They will be either implemented to the glory and honor of God or they will be weapons in the hand of the enemy of all that is good, righteous, and true.

Professor Intellect wants us to think of mental capacity as a muscle. The more it is exercised, the stronger it becomes. How it is exercised determines whether the outcome will be for the good or for evil. There have been countless men and women throughout the ages who have been blessed with tremendous intellects, but they have surrendered them to the powers of darkness and have become infamous for their deranged and criminal genius. As the United Negro College Fund motto states, "the mind is a terrible thing to waste." There are numerous ways to "waste" the mind. The mind is wasted not only by not doing anything at all to develop it, but it is also wasted by not developing it in a way that will bring glory and honor to our Creator. As the songwriter Raymond Rasberry so aptly stated, "Only what you will do for Christ will last".

Our instructor wants us to grasp the next crucially vital intellect principle: the mind only functions correctly if it is constantly pressed, strained, challenged to operate at its highest capacity. In short, it must be trained to always give its all, its best. This principle is Divine in origin and is articulated clearly in various places in God's written word, the Bible. Let us prayerfully consider Matthew 22:37:

Jesus said unto him, Thou shalt love the Lord thy God with all thy heart, and with all thy soul, and with all thy mind.

We must not miss what we just read. It requires all our heart, soul, and *mind* to surrender our gifts and talents completely to the Lord. Stated another way, it requires all our physical, emotional, spiritual, as well as *mental* powers to achieve all that God placed you on this earth to be.

There is an intellect building exercise and principle Professor Intellect always shares with the class. It is found in Philippians 4:8 and is a powerful tool in assisting students who desire to strengthen their minds and increase their mental capacity. Prayerfully consider the following:

Finally, brethren, whatsoever things are true, whatsoever things are honest, whatsoever things are just, whatsoever things are pure, whatsoever things are lovely, whatsoever things are of good report; if there be any virtue, and if there be any praise, think on these things.

Our mental muscle must not only be exercised but it must also be nourished. What we feed our mind determines the direction it will go. Therefore, the admonition of Philippians 4:8 is to make sure that the things we think about are things that will strengthen and improve the highest thoughts and motives as opposed to giving power to the lower or baser thoughts that only bring glory and attention to self, and thereby glory and attention to the enemy of all that is good, righteous, and holy.

Memorization is a powerful tool for enhancing and increasing the capacity of the intellect. Memorization generally falls into one of two categories and it is extremely important that we learn these two fundamental memorization principles. The first and most obvious form of memorization is when we actively seek, practice and strive to memorize. There are various methods for accomplishing this, but at the foundation of them all is the conscious and deliberate effort to memorize specific information. The second form of memorization is the one that comes not from effort but by continual repetition and exposure. If we listen to it long enough, if we are exposed to it long enough, it *will* become a part of us. When under the guidance of the Holy Spirit, this is a tremendous memorization methodology, but the enemy of our souls also has access to this powerful medium of memorization and utilizes it to his greatest advantage whenever possible. Students, we all must be clear that it is Christ's way to, whenever possible, expose Himself *only* to that which will take the thoughts heavenward and not anywhere else. The music we listen to, the programs and movies we watch, the books we read, the conversations we allow in our presence if not consciously resisted, will find a permanent resting place in our memories, in our minds and begin to shape and mold our words, actions, and character. Christ understood that the battle is in the mind and He showed us through His flawless life how to be victorious. Christ constantly and conscientiously applied the principle found in Proverbs 4:23 which counsels us to:

Keep thy heart with all diligence; for out of it are the issues of life.

In Scripture to keep means to guard. In Genesis 3:24 we see that God placed an angel at the entrance of the Garden of Eden after He removed Adam and Eve to keep or to guard or to protect the entrance to the garden which housed the tree of life. In Psalms 91:11 God tells us that He will give His angels charge over us to keep or protect or to guard us in all our ways. Therefore, the admonition in Proverbs 4:23 is to guard our hearts, or our minds, because all the issues of life have their origin in the mind. One interpretation of Proverbs 4:23 reads "guard the avenues to the soul." As conscientious stewards of the intellect that comes from God, it is our solemn and sacred responsibility to make sure that nothing detrimental comes down the street, the road, the path, that leads to our mind. This is the *only* way that we can keep our minds, keep our intellect free from the marring influences of the evil one. Even if we possess an unbelievably high IQ(Intelligence Quotient), even if we make A's in all our classes, even if we have multiple degrees - if the mental capacity has not been surrendered to the softening influence of the Holy Spirit, our intellect will be nothing more than a vehicle in the hands of the wicked one, an instrument of evil instead of an instrument of righteousness.

As the Apostle Paul states, *"For what shall it profit a man, if he shall gain the whole world, and lose his own soul"* (Mark 8:36)

If we don't train and cultivate our intellect, our mental capacity, our brain power to be used in the service of our Saviour Jesus Christ, who came down to this wicked world to live, die, rise and therefore be qualified to be our Advocate in Heaven and stand between us and the ultimate penalty for sin, then it is as if we have done absolutely nothing with the gift. It will be recorded in the books of Heaven that we buried our talent in the ground and did not improve it at all. We must allow the convicting, still, small voice of the Holy Spirit to deeply impress our heart, mind, and soul of the following truth: The only way we can learn of Christ's will, way, and love is to surrender our hearts, our minds, our intellect completely to the only One who gave His life so we could do it–Christ Himself. The object lesson that Instructor Intellect so earnestly longs for us to comprehend is *who* and *what* we let shape and mold our minds will determine our ultimate destiny in this world and the world to come. We must choose wisely. Class dismissed.

Lessons from Intellect:

- I am what I think.
- There is a very real connection between what we think and who we are.
- Whoever controls the intellect controls the entire being.
- Mental capacity is like a muscle. The more it is exercised, the stronger it becomes.
- How mental capacity is exercised determines whether God or Satan will receive the glory.
- The mind is wasted not only by doing nothing to develop it, but also by not developing it in a way that will bring glory and honor to God.
- The mind only functions correctly when it is trained to operate at its highest capacity always.
- Our mental muscle must not only be exercised, it must also be nourished.
- What we feed our minds determines the direction in which they will go.
- Memorization is a powerful tool for increasing the power of the intellect.

- That which we consistently allow ourselves to be exposed to impacts our minds and characters.
- We must guard diligently all avenues to our minds.
- High intelligence cannot prevent the enemy of our souls from marring our mental capacities. Only the Holy Spirit can help us.
- Who and what we allow to shape and mold our minds will determine our ultimate destiny.

Health and Strength

We're to strive to all be healthy, fitness is the goal.

Not just in certain areas, God wants us to be whole.

We're divided into sections, the inner and what's without.

The natural and the spirit, is what this is all about.

We can't be healthy in our bodies while disregarding our mind.

To take this approach will only leave us woefully left behind.

We must incorporate the two, treat them as a team.

When joined they will accomplish more than you could ever dream.

A healthy mind is a healthy soul, it makes you emotionally sound,

And emotional health will truly enable your physical health to abound.

Strength is connected to the mind, it's important that you give your all.

Partial halfhearted effort, will almost guarantee a fall.

You must approach this sacred trust with everything you are

Please do not aim low, set your sights on the highest star.

Your health and strength are gifts from God, He does expect your best.

So, give it your all, do all you can, and God will do the rest.

Derek Arthur Sharpe

Health and Strength

Students, we will now experience something slightly different as we continue our "Learn of Me" journey. Our next class will be team taught. Team teaching is a common education practice; it simply means that more than one teacher teaches the course. With the team teaching dynamic, each instructor presents a topic that can be the same or related to the topics that are being discussed. In our case, two wonderful instructors will share insight into two important topics. The teachers are siblings, both very experienced and both with information that is indispensable for those who wish to have an accurate grasp on just how to learn the ways, will, and love of Christ. I introduce Professor Health and Professor Strength. Professor Health will stand before you first. She likes to begin her class with the scripture principle found in 3 John 2, This scripture is one of the foundational principles of the class: *Beloved, I wish above all things that thou mayest prosper and be in health, even as thy soul prospereth.*

Professor Health emphasizes this critical point at the very onset of her lecture. There are two things that are directly connected to prosperity and both fall under the category of health. Each person in this world has two components to their health—physical health, of which most are aware, and the equally important element of spiritual health. God informs us in this verse that what He desires for every one of His children *above everything else* is that we prosper and have an abundance of physical and spiritual health. The two are intrinsically connected and cannot be separated. No matter how physically fit we are, if there is not a corresponding fitness in our soul, in our spirit, there will be an imbalance that will *always* prove to be detrimental. A healthy mind clears the way for a healthy spirit, but a clear way doesn't guarantee that the clear path will be taken. Taking care of our physical and spiritual health is a choice we must make. Instructor Health cannot emphasize strongly enough that the condition of our physical health has a tremendous impact on not only every aspect of our literal physical power and strength but is critically important to our mental stability and wholeness as well. When our bodies are not in optimal health, our mental capacity is proportionately affected in an adverse manner. Instructor Health would have each of us to understand that the dynamic of health cannot be attended to spasmodically or haphazardly. There must be a clear, decided and determined effort to cultivate and maintain health as a part of life. Psalms 67:2 gives us this important revelation: *That thy way may be known upon earth, thy saving health among all nations.*

Scripture often employs the state-restate method to define and reiterate a concept. In this case, David under inspiration first declares "That Thy way may be known upon earth" and then proceeds to make clear or redefine just what God's way is—saving health. David reveals that our physical or spiritual health cannot be considered *God's health* unless it is directly connected to our salvation. Anything that does not acknowledge the God of Heaven and Earth as the Sovereign of the Universe cannot be classified as health that God endorses.

Another aspect or principle that is revealed in Psalms 67:2 is that 'saving health' is God's way. In Scripture, the word "way" has to do with the character, the very essence of the methodology employed. In Exodus 33:13,18 Moses ask

God to show him *His way* and then restates the same request by asking God to show him *His glory*. In Exodus 34:5-7 God answers Moses request by proclaiming *the Name of the Lord*. Verses six and seven then list the various characteristics of God. Thus, a wonderful revelation is unveiled. *God's way, glory, and name represent His character*. Character is who we are; it is how we operate. It is the default mechanism that kicks in unconsciously, without any thought being employed at all. To speak of our way is to address our character makeup, the very essence of how we go about doing what we do. It speaks to the nature of the methodologies used to accomplish any given goal. Instructor Health really wants each of us to fully grasp this point. Health must be "saving" in nature because the reason or purpose of health is to prepare the body to be the temple or dwelling place for God Himself. This is what is revealed in various places in Scripture. Let us consider 1 Corinthians 6:19,20 and 1 Corinthians 3:16,17.

19 What? know ye not that your body is the temple of the Holy Ghost which is in you, which ye have of God, and ye are not your own?

20 For ye are bought with a price: therefore, glorify God in your body, and in your spirit, which are God's.1 Corinthians 6:19-20

16 Know ye not that ye are the temple of God, and that the Spirit of God dwelleth in you?
17 If any man defile the temple of God, him shall God destroy; for the temple of God is holy, which temple ye are.1 Corinthians 3:16-17

Spiritually and physically our bodies were created to *house the Spirit of God.* They are *not* our bodies. We should maintain a healthy body and mind *because they are where God lives.* As *stewards*, as *housekeepers* of God's dwelling place, it is essential that we raise our level of awareness as to the kind of house God expects to inhabit. This is what is meant by the phrase saving health. It is indeed God's way *and to learn God's way is to also learn God's will, which always teaches God love.* There is much more Professor Health could share, but for now she is going to yield the floor and allow her brother, Professor Strength to come before you at this time.

Professor Strength is also known as might and ability. Although the levels vary, everyone has strength. It is a gift from the Creator to each one of His human creatures and as such it, too, must be cultivated. Professor Strength wants us to be aware of an insidious class that is being taught by the great enemy of our souls. It is being promoted so enthusiastically that many, many precious souls are being deluded and hindered because of this educational philosophy. What is the class, the concept that is being promoted? It is "Try your best not to have to give your best."

It is the enemy's goal to create an entire nation of individuals who only do enough to get by, who never give their all, whose way and very nature is to hold back, to only give a portion. This is diametrically opposed to the will, the way, and the love of Christ. Christ gave His all and He expects all His children to do the same! Prayerfully consider the principle that is articulated in Ecclesiastes 9:10:

Whatsoever thy hand findeth to do, do it with thy might; for there is no work, nor device, nor knowledge, nor wisdom, in the grave, whither thou goest.

Professor Strength cannot emphasize this point enough. *Whatsoever* is an all-inclusive, comprehensive term. *Everything* that we do must be done utilizing our very best effort or else we begin to cultivate the habit, the way, the custom, the character of laziness and halfhearted service. *God expects our very best all the time.* Why is it so very important to do our best, to employ all your strength, all the time? There are many reasons, but there are two that are of the greatest importance. The first is what *we do all the time becomes habit and our habits determine our destiny.*

Guard your thoughts, because thoughts determine your words.

Guard your words, because words determine your actions.

Guard your actions, because actions determine your habits.

Guard your habits, because habits determine your character.

Guard your character because character determines your destiny.

This quote has been ascribed to Frank Outlaw, Ralph Waldo Emerson, and a host of other people. Regardless of who said it, its true source is God, because *it is true* and any and everything that is true and good comes from God! Proverbs 23:7 tells us that "as a man thinketh in his heart so is he." Doing our best is a mindset and according to the above-mentioned quotation, we speak according to what is in our minds and those words ultimately become habits and those habits become character, and our eternal salvation is based upon the type of character we have cultivated.

The second reason to do our best with all our strength and might is just as important as the first. It is impossible to learn the way of Christ, the will of Christ, and the love of Christ when we refuse to give our best or our all. The very essence of who Jesus is, the ingredient that truly personifies and portrays the epitome of His righteousness is, giving His all. The Father emptied heaven to save fallen man. Probably one of the most well-known and well-loved Scriptures in the Bible reminds us of this very fact. John 3:16 keeps ever before us: *For God so loved the world, that he gave his only begotten Son, that whosoever believeth in him should not perish, but have everlasting life.*

There are many operative words and phrases in this powerful scripture, but Professor Strength wants us to focus on two powerful words — *only begotten*. The Father didn't have a dozen sons, nor even three sons, not even two sons. He had only One and He chose to give His one and only Son so that ungrateful, unthankful, unappreciative human beings could at least have the opportunity to be saved from the penalty and ultimate consequences of sin. And He did it fully aware that most of His human creation would spurn the gift and choose the lake of fire over eternal life with Jesus. God gave His best even when He knew it would not be appreciated. Why? Because *that* is the will, the way, and the love of Christ, which is the love of God. So much rides on this principle. When we do not give our all, it impacts our love for God. We are commanded to love God with all we have, and we are truly hindered from doing this when it is not our habit to do anything with all we have. In Matthew 22:37-40, Christ told us that the very foundation of the law is loving with all our ability. Please prayerfully consider what God tells each one of His people in Matthew 22:37-40:

37 Jesus said unto him, Thou shalt love the Lord thy God with all thy heart, and with all thy soul, and with all thy mind.

38 This is the first and great commandment.

39 And the second is like unto it, Thou shalt love thy neighbour as thyself.

40 On these two commandments hang all the law and the prophets.

Jesus used Deuteronomy 6:5 as His springboard scripture. Centuries earlier, Moses was inspired to say the same thing: *And thou shalt love the Lord thy God with all thine heart, and with all thy soul, and with all thy might.*

There is no contradiction between the two scriptures. Christ was emphasizing that it starts in the mind. To do something, anything with all our might, we must first have a mindset to do and give our all. If we do not cultivate the habit of maintaining good health habits and strength habits, our eternal destiny could be at stake and our quality of life will never be lived at its optimum level. As Professor Health joins her brother, they both would like you to know it has been a joy standing before you. It is their sincere desire that you take the principles they presented to you and allow God to show you how to implement them in your lives, so you will indeed be that much closer to knowing the will, the way, and the love of Christ. Class dismissed.

Lessons from Health and Strength:

- Our health consists of two components – physical and spiritual.
- God desires above anything else that His children prosper in physical and spiritual health.
- A healthy mind clears the way for a healthy spirit and a healthy body.
- Physical and Spiritual health require a determined choice.
- When our bodies are not in optimal health, our mental capacity is proportionately affected.
- Health can only be considered God ordained if it is connected to our salvation.
- God's way, His glory, His name, all represent His character.
- Although the levels vary, everyone has strength.
- It is contrary to the will of God to strive to only do enough to get by, to not do your best.

- Doing our best is a habit that must be cultivated, just as not doing our best becomes habitual as well.

- We are to do and give our best even when we know or suspect that it will not be appreciated.

- What we do all the time becomes habit and habits have a great influence upon our eternal destiny.

- When we do not give our all, it impacts our love for God.

Money

From a worldly point of view, it answers everything.

It is considered the wonderful fountain from which all
happiness springs.

The love of it has been the ruin of many great and small.

To get rich quick is the clarion voice to which many have
answered its call.

But money in and of itself is neither good nor bad.

The acquisition or lack thereof should not make us happy or sad.

Money is a gift from God, a talent from above.

No matter what the quantity, its goal is to show His love.

But though it comes from God we can indeed misuse it.

In truth the majority on this earth have chosen to abuse it.

It can be a blessing but also a curse, to hoard it selfishly is a shame.

It brings reproach on God Himself and His dear, precious,
benevolent Name.

The Biblical principle, the Divine rule, that each of us must
come to know-

What's done with a little does unerringly declare which way that you
will choose to go.

He that is faithful in that which is least will be faithful in that
which is much.

God is looking for steadfast stewards, make sure that He
finds you such.

Derek Arthur Sharpe

Money

O ur next instructor has a very unusual reputation. He is extremely misunderstood and is looked down upon by many who profess to be children of God. His class is vital to the Learn of Me curriculum. Indeed, a person cannot truly and completely embrace the will, the way, and the love of Christ without a thorough knowledge of the principles that are found in this class. I introduce Professor Money. Instructor Money begins his lesson with the following scripture found in Ecclesiastes 10:19 which states: *A feast is made for laughter, and wine maketh merry: but money answereth all things.*

Despite the obvious words in the scripture above, money is not and never has been the answer to all things. Verse five of this chapter states that there are errors that proceed from rulers who are not connected to God and therefore unwise in all their thought processes. The concept that money is the answer for all things is one of the errors that proceed from the unwise ruler. Furthermore 2 Kings 5 tells the story of Naaman. Naaman was very rich, but Naaman was a leper. All his money could not cure him, but the power of God did! Likewise, in the New Testament in Luke 18 the story is told of the rich young ruler who realized that something was lacking in his life even though he was extremely rich. Jesus told him what would supply the lack and he was not willing to follow Christ's counsel and left sorrowful. Money is *not* the answer to all things. Christ makes it very clear – without ME ye can do nothing.(John 15:5). Indeed, we all would do well to remember the sobering admonition found in 1 Timothy 6:10 which warns:

For the love of money is the root of all evil: which while some coveted after, they have erred from the faith, and pierced themselves through with many sorrows.

Money, or means, in and of itself is a thing of the world and we are commanded not to love the things of the world. (1 John 2:15-17) Therefore, it is the solemn obligation of all who are in possession of money or means, be the quantity small or large, to regard themselves as stewards of a gift or talent from God because–although it is true that it is a thing of the world–it comes under the authority and possession of God.

Psalms 24:1 informs us that "the earth is the Lord's and the fullness thereof, the world and they that dwell therein." Everything on this planet belongs to God. Men have corrupted His possession, misused an abused His possession, used His possession for wicked and abominable purposes, but nonetheless, at its point of origin, it is the Lord's. Money in and of itself is neither good nor bad, wicked or holy. It is *the use* of money or *the user* of money that determines whether it will support the Lord's kingdom or the enemy's. Money can do great good and it can do great evil. The purpose of this lesson is to impress upon the minds of each of us the sacred and solemn obligation God has given us to make sure that we rely implicitly upon the leading of the Holy Spirit to instruct us in the wise stewardship of the means placed in our hands.

Professor Money will use three passages in Proverbs to expound upon our next monetary principle:

Labour not to be rich: cease from thine own wisdom.
Proverbs 23:4

A faithful man shall abound with blessings: but he that maketh haste to be rich shall not be innocent.
Proverbs 28:20

He that hasteth to be rich hath an evil eye, and considereth not that poverty shall come upon him.
Proverbs 28:22

The recurring theme is clear. It cannot be the goal, aim, or purpose of a Christian to get rich or wealthy. To have such a purpose is to (1) rely on our own wisdom instead of God's; (2) make ourselves "guilty" in the sight of God; and finally (3) to cause us to possess an evil understanding and ultimately place ourselves in the condition we were seeking so ardently to avoid. Money is to be viewed as a tool, an instrument to be used to make others happy, to relieve suffering, to provide opportunities to the disadvantaged, joy to the sorrowing and ultimately to bring a knowledge of our loving Saviour to those who are ignorant of who He truly is.

One of the most important lessons that Professor Money teaches is how we use our money is an accurate barometer of our understanding of the will of the Creator. It is vitally important that you understand what was just stated because it will be extremely beneficial to how your view of others impacts your way of addressing them. Everyone who does unwise or even wicked things with money is not to be condemned. There are many who have not been exposed to the principles of this course. They are unconsciously ignorant, not willfully in defiance of God's laws. We must always consider the two principles of Christ as we deal with our fellow man in the way in which He so lovingly deals with us. Prayerfully consider the following two scriptural principles:

Therefore, to him that knoweth to do good, and doeth it not, to him it is sin. James 4:17 And *the times of this ignorance God winked at; but now commandeth all men every where to repent. Acts 17:30*

God does not hold individuals accountable for that which they do not know. More accurately, God does not hold individuals accountable for that which they have not had an opportunity to know. There are instances where God has orchestrated light to shine in a person' life, but that individual does not take advantage of the opportunity. God is a wise and just judge. It is best to leave that up to Him. Our job is to make sure that in our dealings with others we are displaying the will, the way, and the love of the Saviour. How we dispense our means is one of the best ways to show others exactly that. It is important that we see and understand the huge battle, the tremendous struggle, the great controversy that is raging between the forces of good and the forces of evil. One of the foundational attributes of God is unselfishness. Therefore, one of the foundational attributes of the evil one is selfishness, self-centeredness, being consumed with one's own needs and desires. The talent/gift that God has entrusted to each human being who grows old enough to have it placed in their possession is money. The use of money has the powerful potential of displaying God's unselfishness as few other talents can. Disinterested benevolence, the giving to another purely and solely for the betterment of another, for the joy of another, for the advancement of another with absolutely no benefit to one's self, *that*, is the love of God, it is the way of God, it *is*, His will. God wants us to use this gift with no strings attached, no hidden motive that will ultimately bring gain or recognition to ourselves. Our motive should be the happiness of others. This is the true potential and power of money. Many people find Mark 10:23-27 troubling, so it is necessary we deal with it here.

23 And Jesus looked round about, and saith unto his disciples, How hardly shall they that have riches enter into the kingdom of God!

24 And the disciples were astonished at his words. But Jesus answereth again, and saith unto them, Children, how hard is it for them that trust in riches to enter into the kingdom of God!

25 It is easier for a camel to go through the eye of a needle, than for a rich man to enter into the kingdom of God.

26 And they were astonished out of measure, saying among themselves, Who then can be saved?

27 And Jesus looking upon them saith, With men it is impossible, but not with God: for with God all things are possible.

It is important to note the context of this passage of scripture. Jesus had just finished telling the Rich Young Ruler that the one thing he lacked to gain eternal life was to sell all that he had, give it to the poor, and follow Jesus. Verse 22 states that he left sorrowful, unable to obey Christ's command, because he had great riches. As we transition to verse 23, we must pay very close attention to what Jesus says– It will be *hard* for those who *have* riches to enter the kingdom of God. Then, Jesus repeats Himself– It is *hard* for those who *trust in riches* to enter the kingdom of God. Then, Jesus gives an analogy. The analogy depicts the impossible scenario of a real life, full grown camel attempting to pass through the eye of a sewing needle. Verse 27 is Christ's summation of the analogy, *with men,* when we rely upon human strength and accomplishment, it is impossible for a camel to pass through the eye of a needle or for a rich man to enter heaven, but not with God. *With God all impossibilities are possible.* If we believe that the money we possess is *our* money and not *God's* money entrusted to us, we cannot surrender completely to God's will. That is why Jesus said it was impossible for a rich man to be saved. However, because of the powerful grace of God, the melting, softening influence of the Holy Spirit *can* change the disposition of even the greediest and most selfish among us and give them a mindset that acknowledges God as the supreme owner of the money that is in their possession and allow GOD to lead, guide and direct them as to how it should be used. It is also important to note that this is not a principle that applies only to those who have great wealth. A person can have the selfish mindset of the Rich Young Ruler and not even have much money! It is not about the amount of money, be it great or insignificant, it is the mindset of the individual that matters. A person can be just as selfish and greedy with one dollar as they can be with a million dollars. The mindset, the attitude of the individual, is what our Savior addresses. Let us remember Proverbs 23:7 – how a person thinks, is how that person is. If we think selfishly about the money we possess, then it is because we are selfish. If we are constantly thinking of how we can benefit others with the money entrusted to us, how we can bring glory and honor to our Heavenly Father through the use of the means that is in our power, then it is because we are well on our way to having truly learned of Christ, His will, His way, and His love. May we all, by the grace and power of God, strive to adopt the mindset of Heaven as it relates to the funds that come into our possession. As with some of the other classes, there will be additional courses on finance that will be offered later in the Learn of Me School of Higher Education. For now, you are dismissed.

Lessons from Money:

- Money is not the answer to everything.
- Jesus is the answer to everything.
- The love of money is the root of all evil.
- All money, all wealth belongs to God.
- We are stewards of God's money.
- Money in and of itself is neither good nor bad.
- It should not be the goal or aim of a Christian to be wealthy.
- Money is to be viewed as a tool to relieve the suffering of others and to bring them to a knowledge of Jesus.
- How we use our money is an accurate barometer as to our understanding of God's will.
- How we dispense our means is an excellent way to display the will, the way, and the love of God.
- How we use money has the potential of displaying God's unselfishness to the world.
- It is imperative that we accept the fact that all money is God's and He instructs us as to how to use it.
- If we think it is our money, we can never truly surrender to the will of God.

- A person can have a small amount of money and still manifest the selfishness of the rich young ruler.
- It is never about the amount of money. It is about the mindset of the individual regarding the money.

Kindness and Affection

Rarely are they viewed as talents, gifts rendered from above.

Just as important as grace and mercy, longsuffering, peace and love.

Some could argue they are the foundation of all the other fruit,

For without this pair, to a large extent, the others all are moot.

It is not just that you do a thing, it matters how the thing is done.

It is often the case twas the kindness shown that
was where the battle was won.

Too often taken for granted, not seen as important or needed,

But the absence of kindness and affection is why counsel
goes often unheeded.

Both need to be cultivated, more time must be set aside.

For no matter the sphere, environment or place,
these two elements must abide

Deep within the heart and soul, second nature they must be.

In all circumstances the heart must be trained to see

The places where kindness is needed, the entrance
for affection to get in.

For often tis how the victory's gained, this is how we must learn to win.

Kindly impulses and affections, they most definitely have their place

In helping us all achieve our goal of seeing our Saviour's face.

Derek Arthur Sharpe

Kindness and Affection

This is our final team-taught course. Although they are not related, these two instructors have known each other their entire life and are almost inseparable. Although not related by blood, they consider themselves sisters and are an example of the scripture that tells us that there is "a friend that is closer than a brother"(Proverbs 18:24). Indeed, these two ladies could not be any closer if they were related. They are Professors Kindness and Affection.

Professor Kindness will come before you first. The *Webster's* 1828 edition of the dictionary defines kindness thusly:

KINDNESS, n. [from kind, the adjective.]
1. Good will; benevolence; that temper or disposi-
tion which delights in contributing to the happiness

of others, which is exercised cheerfully in gratifying their wishes, supplying their wants or alleviating their distresses; benignity of nature. Kindness ever accompanies love.

There is no man whose kindness we may not sometime want, or by whose malice we may not sometime suffer.
2. Act of good will; beneficence; any act of benevolence which promotes the happiness or welfare of others. Charity, hospitality, attentions to the wants of others, and, are deemed acts of kindness, or kindnesses. Acts.28.

A portion of the definition states that it is a "temper or disposition," which is a mindset or way of thinking and maybe actually a way of living, that delights in contributing to the happiness of others *and* it does so cheerfully. The definition adds that it also includes supplying of wants and the alleviating of needs, cheerfully and willingly. This is what kindness is. What a very large percentage of the people in this world do not realize is that kindness, being kind, is a gift/talent from the Lord that *He expects* each one of us to cultivate just as earnestly as we cultivate our other talents/

gifts! God requires kindness from all who call themselves His children. The sad truth of the matter is that those who are the unkindest are often those who profess to be followers of our Lord and Saviour Jesus Christ. This might shock some of us, so Instructor Kindness will take us to the source of all wisdom and truth, the origin of all that is just and righteous and good, the Bible, our textbook. We will prayerfully consider God's *command* found in Ephesians 4:32 which reads:

And be ye kind one to another, tenderhearted, for-giving one another, even as God for Christ's sake hath forgiven you.

Instructor Kindness wants us to note, although she is not going to spend much time dealing with it right now, that kindness and forgiveness go hand in hand. I cannot be kind if I refuse to forgive. Stated another way, kindness is the attribute that paves the way for a tender heart that paves the way for the ability to forgive. That is an entirely different class that she teaches, but it needed to at least be pointed out. As Sovereign of the universe, it is important to remember that God does not give suggestions. We cannot disregard anything He says. His words are not optional. If

He said it, we, by His might and in His power, must do all in our power to do it. God said, "Be ye kind one to another." Kindness is one of the foundational elements, one of the essential ingredients, to learning the will, way, and love of Christ. Kindness is power. What makes kindness so powerful? Kindness can soften hard words. Kindness can make difficult situations easier to bear. Kindness can elevate a seemingly insignificant act to a level of great importance. That is why kindness is so important, because it is so very powerful! An example of this is found in one of the most important chapters in the Bible, 1 Corinthians 13, which happens to be the most comprehensive expose' on the true nature of Godly love in the entire Bible. Many people have read and/or heard this passage, but Professor Kindness, as only she can, brings a perspective to one of the passages in this chapter that truly paints kindness in a different light. Let us consider 1 Corinthians 13:4 "Charity suffereth long and is kind." Longsuffering is patience. In James 1:4 patience is said to be "the perfecter" – "let patience have her "perfect work." In Revelation 14:12 when God identifies the group of people that will be on the earth at the time of His return, the attribute that John is inspired to use to describe this illustrious group is patience. Patience is a powerful characteristic. But it is not enough to be longsuffering or patient. The Scripture admonition is to be longsuffering *and kind*. Kindness is what makes the patience effective! If someone is "bearing long" with us, but their disposition is unkind–arms folded, a frowning countenance– although they are waiting, although they are "bearing long," although they are "suffering long," their patience is nullified because they are not being kind. Kindness is the power behind patience and longsuffering! As we continue in the vein of kindness being power, it is important to also view kindness as a muscle. A muscle is indeed powerful, but the extent of its power is contingent upon the exercise and cultivation of the muscle. We do not exercise our kindness muscle nearly enough. Each of us pass up countless opportunities every day to be kind to both those we know and strangers.

There is another dynamic of kindness that is essential to this course and that is the dynamic of family order or the "concept of closeness." Family order, also known as the concept of closeness(which are phrases that Professor Kindness has coined herself) is the principle that is found in 1 Timothy 5:8 and is violated by almost the entire human population: *But if any provide not for his own, and specially for those of his own house, he hath denied the faith, and is worse than an infidel.*

Scripture is plain. Whatever we provide, if we don't provide for our families first, if we don't provide it for those in our household first, according to scripture we have denied the faith and are worse than an infidel, an unbeliever! Unfortunately, this world advocates that we smile and treat those we don't even know with kindness and patience and then come home and be unkind and impatient to those who love us the most. This is straight from the pit of the enemy of our souls! Kindness must begin at home or it is not going to have the power God intended it to have. What is the lesson we must grasp? Often, what you do is not as important as how you do it. The goal is to allow God to bring us to the point where kindness is impulsive, as natural as breathing. Then, we will have truly learned of the Master, and His will, His way, and His love will be seen in all we say and do.

It is now time to transition to Professor Affection.

Professor Affection's presentation is a continuation of Professor Kindness' course. It can be said that kindness is the spiritual or intangible, unseen part, and affection is the physical, tangible, visible part. In short, affection is the physical, "touchy" side of kindness. There is much more to affection than touching, but this is the aspect of affection we are now focusing on. First, we must establish that affection begins in the mind. It is a state of mind. We cannot be affectionate if we do not have affection in our heart and soul. To act with affection without having it in our hearts, results in a merely mechanical operation that does not have the effect and impact that it is supposed to have. Let us all turn to Romans 12:10: *Be kindly affectioned one to another with brotherly love; in honour preferring one another;*

Did you see the close connection between kindness and affection? Even the Bible acknowledges the wonderful relationship they share! There are two extremely important lessons here. Affection must be controlled by God. When the Scriptures tell us to be "kindly affectioned" one to another with brotherly love, it is cautioning us to not allow our affections to be controlled by the evil one. Our affections can be used for good or for evil, and it is of utmost importance that we keep them surrendered to the promptings and leadings of the Holy Spirit. The second principle is just as important. For affection to work the way God intended it to work, it must be unselfish. It must be considered an honor and privilege to bestow affection upon the target or recipient of our affection. The Bible tells us that we must prefer, or give preference to, the needs of others over ours. This affection is entirely different from the low-level affection that is displayed in the world, in the media, and virtually everywhere we look. This is the affection of God, a high and holy affection that transcends that which is carnal and elevates and empowers a hug or embrace, a handshake or even a touch. Just like kindness, affection is powerful! It is important that we allow the Holy Spirit to empower us to "point our affections in the right direction." Colossians 3:1-3 provides further insight:

1 If ye then be risen with Christ, seek those things which are above, where Christ sitteth on the right hand of God.

2 Set your affection on things above, not on things on the earth.

3 For ye are dead, and your life is hid with Christ in God.

The principal point is that we must set our affection on things above, not on things on the earth. There is an unfortunate reality we encounter in the world, "many people spend their life, loving things and using people;" the opposite should be true. We should love people and use things. This is the directional concept that was previously discussed. It is the duty, the obligation, the command of every child of God to set or direct their affection on things of a heavenly, spiritual nature and not on the mundane, temporary things of the earth. What is equally important is that both the verse before and the verse that follows make it very clear that this can only be done when we have died to self and allowed God to make us anew. Affection setting, affection directing, is no small accomplishment. It requires determination, surrender and endurance. We have become accustomed to allowing some of our affections to be directed towards earthly things, so it requires patience to gradually remove all our affections from the things of this earth.

One hymn reminds us that we must "turn our eyes upon Jesus, look full in His wonderful face, and the things of earth will grow strangely dim, in the light of His glory and grace." That is the secret to success as it relates to our affections. The more time we spend looking at Jesus and the things of Jesus, the less attraction the things of this world will hold for our affections. God wants us to be able and willing to direct our affections towards people, not things. *God gave us the talent/ gift of affection to bless people, to help people, to encourage people, to enlighten and empower people.* This is the way of

Christ, this is His will, and it places His love on display. As we allow God to cultivate and shape and mold our affections we will be one step closer in our journey to learn of Christ. When we think of one, kindness, we should certainly think of the other, affection. Kindness and Affection have left their heavenly imprint on our souls. We will now proceed to your final class in this section. Class dismissed.

Lessons from Kindness and Affection:

- Kindness delights in contributing to the happiness of others and does so cheerfully.
- Kindness is a gift/talent from the Lord and He expects His children to cultivate it just like any other talent.
- God requires kindness from all who call themselves His children.
- Those who profess to be God's children are often the unkindest.
- Kindness and forgiveness go hand in hand. I cannot be kind if I cannot forgive.
- Kindness is power. Kindness is powerful.
- Kindness is what makes patience effective.

- We all need to exercise our kindness muscle much more than we do.

- Kindness must begin at home or it is not going to have the power God intended it to have.

- Often, what you do is not as important as how you do it.

- Affection begins in the mind. It is a state of mind.

- Affection must be controlled by God or it will be controlled by the enemy of our souls.

- For affection to function the way God intended, it must be unselfish.

- It must be considered an honor and privilege to bestow affection on the recipient.

- Godly affection elevates and empowers a hug or embrace, a handshake or even a touch.

- We place our affection on things above and not on things of the earth.

- We must place our affection on people and not things.

- The more time we spend looking at Jesus and the things of Jesus, the less attraction the things of this world will hold for our affections.

Life

We're only here for one moment, footprints in the sands of time.

And we must be ever mindful of that love so rich, sublime,

That paid our ransom, bought our freedom,
gave His life so we could live.

There was absolutely nothing else that Jesus Christ could do or give.

Amidst the cares and dreams and projects, the weight of sorrow,
the joy and bliss,

This one thing we must remember, one salient point we dare not miss.

Through grace our life was given to us, a precious time to
become like Him.

There is no time for passing fancy, fleeting folly, wasteful whim.

Every moment of our existence points us to that final call.

When one question we must answer – did we give to Him our all.

Did we enter into His classroom, learn the treasured lessons taught?

Did our life say we were grateful for all our loving Saviour bought?

See Him on that cruel cross, see the thorns press in His brow.

Does your life declare completely I love my Jesus, I love Him now?

Life is not about tomorrow, what have you given Him today?

Live your life so you are certain, you will be with Him alway!

Derek Arthur Sharpe

Life

This is the last course in this section of the "Learn of Me" curriculum. The final instructor attempts to bring together all that was covered in this section. The instructor is older than the others. He goes by many names, but, aside from his actual name, he is most often associated with the name of Experience. He is Professor Life.

We must embrace that life itself is an object lesson and life itself is full of object lessons. All the other instruction that we have received and will receive in the Learn of Me curriculum falls within the confines of Life. Life is the comprehensive classroom that embraces and embodies all other classrooms. It is impossible for a lesson to be taught, an experience to be learned, a perspective to be gained-without life. Why? Because the Sovereign of the Universe, the Creator of all there is, the sustainer and protector of every living thing is life itself. Jesus Christ *is life*. Let us consider John 1:1-4:

> *In the beginning was the Word, and the Word was with God, and the Word was God.*
>
> *2 The same was in the beginning with God.*
>
> *3 All things were made by him; and without him was not anything made that was made.*
>
> *4 IN HIM WAS LIFE; AND THE LIFE WAS THE LIGHT OF MEN.*

Life itself is located *within* Jesus Christ and that life located within Jesus Christ, also known as the Word of God, is the light of men. This is an important principle– *All life is light, and all light is life*. To put it another way, whenever we find something that is alive or living, it is because it has light in it. This has nothing to do with the color of it, the location of it, the size of it, or any other variables. If it is alive, it must also have light. Conversely, no matter how expensive, no matter how expansive, no matter how great its exposure to light, if it is not alive, it is impossible for it to contain or possess light. This is what lies at the foundation of every object lesson. *Jesus Christ is associated with all that is light, and the enemy of our souls is associated with all that is darkness.* Jesus teaches us this in John 10:10: *The thief cometh not, but for to steal, and to kill, and to destroy: I am come that they might have life, and that they might have it more abundantly.*

It is of the utmost importance that we grasp the message of John 10:10. *No matter what it looks like, sounds like, tastes like, feels like,* if the enemy of our souls is the author of it, the purpose and goal of that thing is fiendishly calculated to steal your life, to extinguish your light, and to destroy your soul. Period. No exceptions to the rule! No matter how alluring, no matter how promising, if Christ is not the author of it, it *will* end in death. Solomon, the wisest king to ever rule, put it this way in Proverbs 14:12: *There is a way which seemeth right unto a man, but the end thereof are the ways of death.*

It seems right to the man or woman who is listening to the deceptive insinuations of the arch apostate who specializes in making things seem or appear to be living, when they are *dead.* It is only the grace and mercy of God that rescues individuals from this path of destruction *before* they get to the end of it, which is guaranteed death. Christ, on the other hand, has a different object in mind for anyone who is willing to accept His counsel, follow His directions, and heed his warnings. The outcome will not only be a life of *life*, but it will be a life lived at the full level of abundance.

It is important to note that the abundant life that Christ promises is not attainable if sin is present. Abundant living does not truly take place until every trace, every evidence, every particle of sin, *along with its author,* is completely and totally removed. *When* that takes place, *because IT IS going to take place,* those who have made the conscious decision to follow the wise counsel and admonition of our Lord, those who have by faith accepted the atoning sacrifice of His precious blood shed on Calvary, they will experience abundant life – eternal life. The seducing lie that has been promulgated upon most unsuspecting humans is that abundance has everything to do with how many things a person possesses, when in reality, abundance, according to the mindset of the Creator, is measured by how long a person has to enjoy what they have. All, everything, that the enemy proposes to give is temporary. His entire kingdom is temporary! Why is this so? Because it does not have life in it. 1 John 2:15-17 and Hebrews 11:24-25 can assist us in grasping this principle:

15 Love not the world, neither the things that are in the world. If any man love the world, the love of the Father is not in him.

16 For all that is in the world, the lust of the flesh, and the lust of the eyes, and the pride of life, is not of the Father, but is of the world.

17 AND THE WORLD PASSETH AWAY, AND THE LUST THEREOF: but he that doeth the will of God abideth forever.1 John 2:15-17

24 By faith Moses, when he was come to years, refused to be called the son of Pharaoh's daughter;

25 Choosing rather to suffer affliction with the people of God, than to enjoy THE PLEASURES OF SIN FOR A SEASON. Hebrews 11:24-25

These biblical passages capture perfectly the nature of the kingdom of this world and everything in it: (1) It passes away, meaning it is not eternal or everlasting and (2) it is seasonal, or it has a beginning point and an ending point. Conversely, John 3:16 is not a promise for a specified, limited period. God promises us that all who believe on the merits of a crucified Savior will obtain, will possess everlasting life! Like Moses, we must cultivate, through God's help, the ability to choose those things that have lasting value and not those things that will perish. In other words, we should learn to cultivate the habit of loving things that are eternal and liking things that are not.

We just read the God-given admonition to refrain from loving the things of this world. Here is a tremendous lesson. If it cannot go with us into the new earth, to love it is detrimental to our soul salvation. Therefore Colossians 3:2 tells us to "set your affection on things above." Because things above are eternal.

The final point Professor Life hopes we understand is the transitional nature of this life. Everything, everything, everything in our lives is divinely designed to transition us back to the Tree of Life! What does the Genesis account teach us? The sinless pair were perfectly fine if they were partaking only of the Tree of Life. The moment they partook of the Tree of Knowledge of Good and Evil they lost the privilege to partake of the Tree of Life. Life stopped for them the moment they ate of the forbidden tree. The life of a Christian consists of gradually allowing the Holy Spirit to wean us off the things pertaining to the Tree of Knowledge of Good and Evil and preparing us to again partake of the Tree of Life. One of your next instructors, Professor Sanctuary, helps us to clearly understand through God's Heavenly visual aid, the actual steps each one of us must take in this Heavenly transition. It includes choices pertaining to our diet, our dress, our entertainment, even our conversation. We will allow Professor Sanctuary to shed more light on that for you, for he is your next class. For now, suffice it to say, everything we do, everything we say, everything we even think, is either helping us or hindering us on our transitional pathway back to the Tree of Life. Philippians 4:8 provides an inspired principle as to the types of things our minds should be feeding upon as we prepare ourselves to again be partakers of the Tree of Life.

Finally, brethren, whatsoever things are true, what-soever things are honest, whatsoever things are just, whatsoever things are pure, whatsoever things are lovely, whatsoever things are of good report; if there be any virtue, and if there be any praise, think on these things. Philippians 4:8

If we allow the Holy Spirit to show us how to apply the principle above to everything we do, we will be well on our way to truly and completely grasping the way, the will, and the love of Christ. The final scripture of the class is Instructor Life's final plea to each student he has ever taught. It is the plea of our Lord and Saviour as well. It is found in Deuteronomy 30: 19:

I call heaven and earth to record this day against you, that I have set before you life and death, blessing and cursing: therefore choose life, that both thou and thy seed may live:

God Himself has placed before each one of us two choices: Life and Death, Blessings and Cursings. He urges us all to choose life. Class dismissed.

Lessons from Life:

- Life itself is an object lesson and life itself is full of object lessons.
- Life itself is located *within* Jesus Christ.
- All life is light, and all light is life.
- Jesus Christ is associated with all that is light, and the enemy of our souls is associated with all that is darkness.

- No matter how alluring, no matter how promising, if Christ is not the author of it, it *will* end in death.

- The abundant life that Christ promises will not be attainable until all sin is forever at an end.

- The world measures abundance in terms of what a person possesses, but God measures abundance based on *how long* a person can enjoy what they have.

- The fundamental nature of this world is it has a beginning point and an ending point. It will pass away.

- God's kingdom has always been and will *never* end.

- We should learn to cultivate the habit of loving things that are eternal and liking things that are not.

- If it cannot go with us into the new earth, to love it is detrimental to our soul salvation.

- Everything in the Christian life is divinely designed to transition us back to the tree of life.

The Sanctuary

It isn't something long ago that matters not today.
It is God's object lesson that shows us all the way.
It's a visual aid par excellence, the ultimate tool to show
The path we all must travel, the way each child must go,
To enter through those pearly gates and hear Him say "well done".
It shows us that the battle with our enemy has been won.
No matter what we've said or done, it shows He will defend.
Christ becomes our Advocate, our Saviour and our Friend.
It teaches us that we must enter through Christ, who is the door,
And as we walk with Jesus, we will love Him more and more.
When it was built upon the earth it wasn't something new,
Its pattern was in heaven, it displayed a perfect view
Of what our High Priest does for us whenever we trip and fall.
He takes our sins before the throne, He takes them one and all,
And cast them deep into the sea as if we have no sin,
And allows us and empowers us to boldly begin again.

Derek Arthur Sharpe

The Sanctuary

Thy way, O God, is in the sanctuary: who is so great a God as our God? Psalms 77:13

We are about to enter a classroom that quite possibly contains the greatest object lesson and Divine visual aid in the entire Bible! Teachers, excellent teachers, understand the importance of utilizing object lessons and visual aids to ensure that their students grasp and retain the principles they are teaching. God is the Master Educator. There is none greater than He, so it would stand to reason that He would make use of these two educational instruments. Let us pay close, prayerful attention as we begin the curriculum that contains Christ's spiritual object lessons contained in the Holy Scriptures. The first lesson is "The Sanctuary." It is of the utmost importance that we comprehend at the very onset what is articulated in this Scripture. In our Nature curriculum we encountered Moses interacting with God (Exodus 33 and 34) and we learned that God's Glory is His Name and His Character. We revisit Exodus 33 now and consider verse 13 as God gives additional insight.

Now therefore, I pray thee, if I have found grace in thy sight, shew me now thy way, that I may know thee, that I may find grace in thy sight: and consider that this nation is thy people

When Moses asked God in verse 18 to show him His glory, he was repeating a question that he had already asked in verse 13. God's way is God's glory and God's glory is God's character. Suddenly, Psalm 77:13 climbs up the priority ladder to the number one place of prominence! It is no longer an Old Testament Scripture that no longer has any bearing on our Christian dispensation. God's character, His way of dealing with erring, sinful, weak, rebellious humanity, is in the sanctuary! And the sanctuary is a visual aid that depicts completely every facet of the plan of salvation! In John 10:9 Jesus teaches us that He is the door. When a penitent sinner enters the door, newly adopted into the family of Christ, the very first lesson comes in the form of a question: Do you love Me enough to die for Me? This question is embodied in the altar of burnt offering. At this point, doctrine is not the most important part. What matters at the foundational stage of the Christian experience is love for Jesus and a willingness to embrace the twofold message of the altar–Christ died for me. Am I willing? Is my love strong enough? Is my appreciation and gratitude deep enough and strong enough to die for Him?

Another very important dynamic is the space that is between each article of furniture and that marks each transition to another level of the Christian's relationship with Jesus. Our great textbook teaches us in Revelation 2:21 that our Saviour gives us "space to repent." Only our Saviour knows just how long it will take for the darkness of our hearts to be won to Him. It is such a blessing that our salvation depends on His timing and not man's. After our dying to self-experience which is a daily encounter with the altar (Luke 9:23), we proceed to the laver, the symbol of baptism, a public washing away of the past and a declaration that we have indeed been "persuaded," though not fully, to follow Jesus on this path of sanctification. After another space we encounter another door. Jesus is still the door and He has yet another question for those who seek entrance into a higher relationship with Him. This time the question is not "do you love Me enough to die for Me, but rather, "do you love Me enough to live for me? The courtyard phase of the Christian experience is a time of establishing firmly the foundation of the Christian walk. So often, individuals neglect this part of the journey, and though they may enter the next phase and may learn all about Jesus, they will not be able to truly establish that next level of relationship with Jesus. They have not decided to give Jesus their all. This unfortunate condition is spoken of in 2 Timothy 3:7–individuals who are "ever learning and never able to come to the knowledge of Christ." That knowledge is gained in the space between the door and the altar, as we allow the cross to truly melt our hearts and convince us –before we even know the total cost– that Jesus' death for us is worth whatever He can ask of us. When the individual has to God's satisfaction been able to answer the second question truthfully and honestly, he or she can enter the Holy Place. This is the phase where the Christian begins to understand what it means to live for Christ. The first thing the individual encounters in the Holy Place is the Table of Shewbread. Now, it is time to begin to eat of Christ, to digest His will and His way. In John 6:35 Jesus says, "I am the bread of life." It is in this phase of the Sanctuary Educational Institution that we begin to learn the doctrines of Christianity. It is in this phase that we come to a better understanding that there must be a distinct difference between the Christian and the one who does not know Christ. The dress, the diet, the lifestyle, the response and reaction to adverse situations, all are markedly different from the approach of those outside of the Sanctuary. Throughout Scripture God calls His people to be separate, to be apart, to be different, to be peculiar even. The following scriptures reiterate this principle.

And that ye may put difference between holy and unholy, and between unclean and clean Leviticus 10:10

Wonder of wonders, God considers us holy and He tells us there must be a difference between that which is holy and that which is unholy.

For from the top of the rocks I see him, and from the hills I behold him: lo, the people shall dwell alone, and shall not be reckoned among the nations Numbers 23:9

God admonishes us that we should not be "reckoned" or "considered" or "counted" among those who do not know the Lord. As to the question of whether we must be separate from the ungodly, God tells us we must dwell "alone."

16 And what agreement hath the temple of God with idols? for ye are the temple of the living God; as God hath said, I will dwell in them, and walk in them; and I will be their God, and they shall be my people.

17 Wherefore come out from among them, and be ye separate, saith the Lord, and touch not the unclean thing; and I will receive you,

18 And will be a Father unto you, and ye shall be my sons and daughters, saith the Lord Almighty.
2 Corinthians 6:16-18

Here we see God clearly relating His will and His way to His people. There must be a separation.

But ye are a chosen generation, a royal priesthood, an holy nation, a peculiar people; that ye should shew forth the praises of him who hath called you out of darkness into his marvellous light: 1 Peter 2:9

Sometimes the things God asks of us will seem to make us peculiar or different, but we must trust that He knows what is best for us.

Finally, in Revelation, the very last book of the Bible, for the last time, God calls His people to come out and be separate from the influences of those that do not want to follow Jesus with all their hearts.

And I heard another voice from heaven, saying, Come out of her, my people, that ye be not partakers of her sins, and that ye receive not of her plagues.
Revelation 18:4

These are the principles we learn as they relate to loving Jesus enough to live for Him. We move from the table of shewbread although–just like the altar of burnt offering–we will partake of it daily. The next item in the Holy Place is the altar of incense. This is where we develop a prayer life with Jesus, not only talking to Him but hearing Him talking to us. Let us consider the purpose of the altar of incense as illustrated in the scripture:

And when he had taken the book, the four beasts and four and twenty elders fell down before the Lamb, having every one of them harps, and golden vials full of odours, which are the prayers of saints. And another angel came and stood at the altar, having a golden censer; and there was given unto him much incense, that he should offer it with the prayers of all saints upon the golden altar which was before the throne.

4 And the smoke of the incense, which came with the prayers of the saints, ascended up before God out of the angel's hand. Revelation 8:3-4

It is in the Holy Place that we learn the much broader application of prayer. Prayer is so much more than just calling on God or even having God speak to you. Prayer is a connection, a communion, a state of always being in the presence of God. This is what 1 Thessalonians 5:17 teaches when it urges us to "Pray without ceasing." A continual, unbroken connection with the Lord is the goal of each Christian that enters the Holy Place. The final article of furniture in our Holy Place journey is the candlestick. It represents our privilege and ability to witness for our Master.

This is the only light source in the Holy Place other than the soft glow that emanates from the Shekinah Glory behind the veil in the Most Holy Place. We are commissioned by Christ to let our light shine for one specific purpose:

Let your light so shine before men, that they may see your good works, and glorify your Father which is in heaven. Matthew 5:16

This principle of witnessing is taught in the following two scriptures:

I have declared, and have saved, and I have shewed, when there was no strange god among you: therefore, ye are my witnesses, saith the Lord, that I am God. Isaiah 43:12

But ye are a chosen generation, a royal priesthood, an holy nation, a peculiar people; that ye should shew forth the praises of him who hath called you out of darkness into his marvellous light. 1 Peter 2:9

It is only in the Holy Place experience that we can be trusted by God to truly represent who God is to a dying world. But there is still one level to go, one more level of Jesus Christ to experience. We are now ready to enter the final door, the final experience with Jesus, and there is one final question that our Saviour has for us. We have agreed to die for Him because we love Him enough to do so. We have agreed to live for Him, because we love Him enough to do so. The final question we must respond to from our Wonderful Counselor, Saviour and King is: "Do you love Me enough to become completely one with Me? Let us take a moment to contemplate the prayer of the Redeemer of the world for us.

19 And for their sakes I sanctify myself, that they also might be sanctified through the truth.
20 Neither pray I for these alone, but for them also which shall believe on me through their word;
21 That they all may be one; as thou, Father, art in me, and I in thee, that they also may be one in us: that the world may believe that thou hast sent me.
22 And the glory which thou gavest me I have given them; that they may be one, even as we are one:

23 I in them, and thou in me, that they may be made perfect in one; and that the world may know that thou hast sent me, and hast loved them, as thou hast loved me. John 17:19-23

It should touch our hearts that the Creator of the universe prayed for us. He prayed that we would be one *with* and *in* Him and the Father. He prayed that we would experience and share the same oneness that He and the Father share. The wonder of it all! This final surrendering, our life for His, is brought out in Galatians 2:20.

I am crucified with Christ: nevertheless I live; yet not I, but Christ liveth in me: and the life which I now live in the flesh I live by the faith of the Son of God, who loved me, and gave himself for me.

We reach a point in our relationship with Christ that we are not living our own lives anymore. Christ lives in us and His faith propels and actuates our lives. *This* is the experience of the Most Holy Place. There is only one article of furniture in this most sacred place – The Ark of The Covenant. Within it are located three things, The Ten Commandments on the two tables of stone that God originally wrote them on, a bowl of the manna with which God fed the children of Israel while they were wandering in the wilderness, and Aaron's rod that blossomed so that all would know that he had been chosen to be God's High Priest even though Korah, Dathan, and Abiram accused him and Moses of being dictators. The location of these three items, in the Ark of the Covenant represent where they must be in the life of the Christian – in our hearts. The Bible teaches that when we allow God to write His law in our hearts, we have accepted fully the calling that He has placed upon our lives. It also teaches that when we hide God's word in our heart, it is not so easy for us to sin. As one of the fundamental needs of life is food, the bowl of manna represents our complete and total confidence, in our hearts, that God will supply all our physical and temporal needs. Just like God performed a miracle to supply the needs of Israel, that same God will supply all our needs as well. And finally, Aaron's rod represents total acceptance in our hearts of whatever God has called us to do. It will not always be easy, but when it is in our heart, obedience to God is not even a thought. Scripture reminds us that God must place His law in our hearts for us to follow Him and for Him to be our God:

For this is the covenant that I will make with the house of Israel after those days, saith the Lord; I will put my laws into their mind and write them in their hearts: and I will be to them a God, and they shall be to me a people. Hebrews 8:10

When God's law is hidden in our hearts, it is not so easy for us to sin:

Thy word have I hid in mine heart, that I might not sin against thee. Psalms 119:11

God has promised to supply all our needs:

But my God shall supply all your need according to his riches in glory by Christ Jesus. Philippians 4:19

Christ specifically promised that our bread and water would be sure:

He shall dwell on high: his place of defence shall be the munitions of rocks: bread shall be given him; his waters shall be sure. Isaiah 33:16

And finally, we must be confident that God has called us:

Wherefore the rather, brethren, give diligence to make your calling and election sure: for if ye do these things, ye shall never fall. 2 Peter 1:10

Scripture tells us it is not enough just to be "called."

These shall make war with the Lamb, and the Lamb shall overcome them: for he is Lord of lords, and King of kings: and they that are with him are called, and chosen, and faithful. Revelation 17:14

Though we have only scratched the surface of this educational tool, we have taken the visual tour of the plan of salvation. In the Sanctuary we find that God gives His people time to reach His high standards. Jesus told us in John 3:3 that the path of the Christian is just like a baby being born and in order to begin the journey, we all must be born again. This means no matter how old we are and what we have accomplished, we will have to start over again as little babies in Jesus. It is in the Sanctuary that we learn that it is not enough to just find a Bible text that advocates that we can or cannot do something. We must find out where that text fits in the Sanctuary. Is it a courtyard requirement? God allows things in the courtyard experience that He does not allow in the succeeding two experiences, just like there are things we are allowed to do when we are three and four years old that we cannot do when we are 15 and 16. And even more is required by the time we are 30 and 40. Consider that Jesus' entire ministry was a courtyard experience. Jesus had a threefold ministry– Prophet, Priest, and King. He came to this earth as a Prophet (Courtyard) He ascended to Heaven as our High Priest (Holy Place) and later on in the Christian dispensation He was crowned King (Most Holy Place). We must see this threefold Prophet, Priest, and King concept in God's word. Let us begin by showing that Jesus was viewed as a prophet the entire time He was on this earth:

And the multitude said, this is Jesus the prophet of Nazareth of Galilee. Matthew 21:11

The people saw Him as a prophet.

And he said, Verily I say unto you, no prophet is accepted in his own country. Luke 4:24

Jesus referred to Himself as a prophet.

And he said unto them, What things? And they said unto him, Concerning Jesus of Nazareth, which was a prophet mighty in deed and word before God and all the people. Luke 24:19

His disciples referred to Him as a prophet till His death. (They did not know that He had risen in this passage.)

Then those men, when they had seen the miracle that Jesus did, said, this is of a truth that prophet that should come into the world. John 6:14

The people were expecting a prophet and proclaimed that Jesus was that prophet.

Now we must see that Jesus is at this very moment, and has been since he ascended to Heaven, acting as our High Priest:

15 For we have not an high priest which cannot be touched with the feeling of our infirmities; but was in all points tempted like as we are, yet without sin.

16 Let us therefore come boldly unto the throne of grace, that we may obtain mercy, and find grace to help in time of need. Hebrews 4:15-16

Christ is our High Priest in Heaven right now.

Wherefore, holy brethren, partakers of the heavenly calling, consider the Apostle and High Priest of our profession, Christ Jesus. Hebrews 3:1

Christ is our High Priest right now.

21 (For those priests were made without an oath; but this with an oath by him that said unto him, The Lord sware and will not repent, Thou art a priest for ever after the order of Melchisedec:)
22 By so much was Jesus made a surety of a better testament. Hebrews 7:21-22

Christ is our High Priest right now.

My little children, these things write I unto you, that ye sin not. And if any man sin, we have an advocate with the Father, Jesus Christ the righteous. 1 John 2:1

As our High Priest, Christ acts and functions as our Advocate/Mediator.

Finally, we see that Christ cannot come back as a prophet, for by the time He returns, there is nothing else for Him to foretell. It will be over. He will not be coming back as our High Priest. He will no longer need to intercede on our behalf. It will be over. He can only return as a conquering King!

15 Which in his times he shall shew, who is the blessed and only Potentate, the King of kings, and Lord of lords;
16 Who only hath immortality, dwelling in the light which no man can approach unto; whom no man hath seen, nor can see: to whom be honour and power everlasting. Amen.1 Timothy 6:15-16

Christ is King!

14 These shall make war with the Lamb, and the Lamb shall overcome them: for he is Lord of lords, and King of kings: and they that are with him are called, and chosen, and faithful. Revelation 17:14

His final war is as King

11 And I saw heaven opened and behold a white horse; and he that sat upon him was called Faithful and True, and in righteousness he doth judge and make war.

12 His eyes were as a flame of fire, and on his head were many crowns; and he had a name written, that no man knew, but he himself.

13 And he was clothed with a vesture dipped in blood: and his name is called The Word of God.

14 And the armies which were in heaven followed him upon white horses, clothed in fine linen, white and clean.

15 And out of his mouth goeth a sharp sword, that with it he should smite the nations: and he shall rule them with a rod of iron: and he treadeth the winepress of the fierceness and wrath of Almighty God.

16 And he hath on his vesture and on his thigh a name written, KING OF KINGS, AND Lord OF Lords. Revelation 19:11-16

His final battle is as the King of Kings and Lord of Lords. Jesus did something that should only be done while we are in the courtyard experience of our walk with the Lord. As soon as you enter our Holy Place experience, naturally the requirements will become more complex because God requires more of those He has given more.

But he that knew not, and did commit things worthy of stripes, shall be beaten with few stripes. For unto whomsoever much is given, of him shall be much required: and to whom men have committed much, of him they will ask the more. Luke 12:48

Our God is a reasonable God. His way is a progressive way. This is what the Sanctuary teaches with its three compartments. Jesus deals with us in stages, in phases, progressively. The Sanctuary is not the only teacher God uses to display this principle. The Holy Bible begins with showing us His Way. God could have spoken the entire world into existence with one word, but He chose to do it in six literal days so that we might know that He is a God of progress and stages. We will close with these final two scriptural passages that reiterate God's wonderful message in the Sanctuary.

26 And he said, So is the kingdom of God, as if a man should cast seed into the ground;

27 And should sleep, and rise night and day, and the seed should spring and grow up, he knoweth not how.

28 For the earth bringeth forth fruit of herself; first the blade, then the ear, after that the full corn in the ear.

29 But when the fruit is brought forth, immediately he putteth in the sickle, because the harvest is come. Mark 4:26-29

God said this is the fundamental characteristic of His Kingdom. See, blade, ear, full corn in the ear. A progressive process just like the Sanctuary advocates.

For as the earth bringeth forth her bud, and as the garden causeth the things that are sown in it to spring forth; so the Lord God will cause righteousness

and praise to spring forth before all the nations.
Isaiah 61:11

The progressive principle is how God adds godly characteristics to our life. We should not fret because we are not perfect Christians overnight. We should not even expect to praise Him the way He deserves to be praised at first. God assures us that in His timing, as we are obedient to His will and His way, His love for us *and* our love for Him will cause both righteousness and praise to mature just like a bud becomes a flower in a garden!

Whew! That was a long class. But it is God's premier showcase, His best lesson, His greatest instrument to display His way, His will and His love.

Lessons from the Sanctuary:

- God's way is God's glory and God's glory is God's character.
- God's character, His way of dealing with erring, sinful, weak, rebellious humanity, is in the sanctuary.
- The sanctuary is a visual aid that depicts completely every facet of the plan of salvation.

- In John 10:9 Jesus teaches us that He is the door.

- When a penitent sinner enters the door, newly adopted into the family of Christ, the very first lesson comes in the form of a question: Do you love Me enough to die for Me?

- What matters at the foundational stage of the Christian experience is love for Jesus and a willingness to embrace the twofold message of the altar—Christ died for me. Am I willing? Is my love strong enough? Is my appreciation and gratitude deep enough and strong enough to die for Him?

- The space between each article of furniture in the Sanctuary represents the time it takes for an individual to accept that phase of God's message.

- The Laver represents baptism, a public declaration that the old life is dead and the new life has been washed by the blood of Jesus and His word.

- In John 6:35 Jesus says, "I am the bread of life.". The eating and digesting of Christ's way of life is symbolized by the table of shewbread.

- The altar of incense represents the prayer life of a Christian.

- The candlesticks represent the witness, or the life that is seen by others, of the Christian.

- The Ark of the Covenant contains the Ten Commandments on tables of stone written by God Himself, a bowl of manna, and Aaron's rod that blossomed.

- Every Christian must believe in their heart that God will supply all of their temporal needs.

- Every Christian must believe in their hearts that what God has called them to do or be is what is best.

- The Ten Commandments can only truly be kept when they are written on the heart of the believer.

- Christ's life and ministry is broken down into three parts: Prophet, Priest, and King. He came as a Prophet. He is now acting as our High Priest, and He will return to get His people as King of Kings and Lord of Lords.

The Pot of Oil

There was nothing really special about the vessels that she chose.
She was just obeying orders, needing solutions for her woes.

A husband dead, a giant bill, a collector and his threat,
She'd lose her boys and lose them now, if she couldn't pay the debt.

She didn't have the money, she had nowhere she could go,
But there was one man that she thought could help,
                    if he wouldn't tell her no.

She gathered all her courage and she went to plead her case.
She needed the prophet Elisha to look into her face.

She knew Elisha knew her husband, knew the caliber of the man,
She was hoping her husband's character would somehow lend a hand

In compelling him to help her out and help is what she got.
The man of God directed her that help was in her pot.

It was not in the directions, it was how much did she believe
She could do what she'd been told to do or continue just to grieve.

Her faith – it was rewarded, and your faith will be rewarded too
As you purpose in your heart by faith to do what you must do.

Derek Arthur Sharpe

The Pot of Oil

Now there cried a certain woman of the wives of the sons of the prophets unto Elisha, saying, Thy servant my husband is dead; and thou knowest that thy servant did fear the Lord: and the creditor is come to take unto him my two sons to be bondmen.

2 And Elisha said unto her, What shall I do for thee? tell me, what hast thou in the house? And she said, Thine handmaid hath not anything in the house, save a pot of oil.

3 Then he said, Go, borrow thee vessels abroad of all thy neighbours, even empty vessels; borrow not a few.

4 And when thou art come in, thou shalt shut the door upon thee and upon thy sons, and shalt pour out into all those vessels, and thou shalt set aside that which is full.

5 So she went from him and shut the door upon her and upon her sons, who brought the vessels to her; and she poured out.

6 And it came to pass, when the vessels were full, that she said unto her son, Bring me yet a vessel. And he said unto her, There is not a vessel more. And the oil stayed.

7 Then she came and told the man of God. And he said, Go, sell the oil, and pay thy debt, and live thou and thy children of the rest. 2 Kings 4:1-7

Before we begin our classroom journey into the New Testament object lessons, we will take one additional course in the Old Testament. A widow, her two sons, a prophet, and a pot of oil join forces through the work of the Holy Spirit to assist us in gathering object lessons which will heighten our understanding of His way, His will, and His love.

Lesson number one: Sometimes there is value in "knowing someone who knows someone." The widow's late husband had been closely connected to Elisha and now, in a time of adversity, she leaned upon her late husband's relationship with the prophet and sought counsel and assistance.

The greater object lesson is that by Divine adoption we are connected to the Holy Spirit, who is connected to Jesus, who is connected to The Father. We benefit completely from Christ's relationship with the Father. (See the entire chapter of John 17, Romans 8:15, Ephesians 1:5)

The widow's late husband left her in debt. The creditor threatened to enslave her two sons until the debt is paid. She went to the man of God for help. His first question is of the utmost significance to us. Whenever we are facing a trial, no matter how great the adversity, the first question we need to consider is "What hast thou in the house?" So often we overlook the very thing that God can and will use for our benefit.

There is a hidden object lesson in the widow's response. *"And she said, Thine handmaid hath not anything in the house, save a pot of oil."* There is a key word in this response that requires a deeper application to truly appreciate the object lesson and gain a better understanding of God's way. She answered I don't have anything, *save* this pot of oil. The pot of oil is about to teach us a valuable lesson. It possesses divine credentials, so don't get distracted because we are being instructed by a pot of oil. Jesus uses many things to teach His people. The surface definition for the word "save" is except. This usage appears in various other places in the scripture. But aside from the natural language application, the pot of oil requires that we look deeper for a surprising object lesson. We should see the word save as *saved* or set aside for a Divine purpose–deliberately overlooked so it could fulfill its Divinely appointed mission. There will be times in our lives when we realize the least likely thing–the thing still hanging around, the thing we thought we had disposed of long ago–has been saved to be the God-given answer to our problems. That is why we have the principle and wonderful assurance of Mark 10:27 which blesses us by reminding us that *"with men it is impossible, but not with God: for with God all things are possible."* The man of God now gives the widow directions that provide us with our next object lesson in the story. She must go to all her neighbors and borrow their empty vessels. What is God trying to teach us? We must be willing to give and to do our all for God to work mightily on our behalf.

In Scripture, oil is closely associated with anointing, and anointing is closely associated with the Holy Spirit. Oil is a symbol or representation of the Holy Spirit. When Saul was anointed king (with oil) the Spirit came upon him (1 Samuel 10:1-11). When Jesus announced the beginning of His ministry, He connected the Spirit of the Lord with the anointing (Luke 4:18). Within this context, God is also striving to let His people know that we must give our all if we are to be filled with His Holy Spirit. Halfhearted service, halfhearted effort will not produce the vessel prepared for the Holy Spirit. Ecclesiastes 9:10 states it thusly, *"Whatsoever thy hand findeth to do, do it with thy might; for there is no work, nor device, nor knowledge, nor wisdom, in the grave, whither thou goest."* It requires all our might, our very best. God accepts nothing less.

There is another just as vital point associated with this portion of the story. Often, God requires a tremendous amount of humility to accomplish a desired request. It was not necessarily easy to go around to every neighbor and ask to borrow a vessel. Humility and perseverance are necessary elements. In short, go low and go all the way! Complete and total obedience meant not leaving out a single neighbor! The wonderful part of the story is that the widow acted in complete faith. The mission was set before her: (1) Go to everybody. The passage uses the word "abroad," which implies not just those in close proximity. (2) Borrow empty vessels. (3) Reiteration and motivation – Borrow not a few. Borrow possibly more than one from each neighbor (4) Why? The purpose would be opened to her if she believes!

The man of God made a ridiculous proclamation. When you have finished obtaining as many vessels as you can possibly find, then begin to fill them all up with your one set aside, saved for this very moment pot of oil. There are individuals who would never even have borrowed one single vessel because the promise seemed impossible. The fact that the widow understood what the prophet said was going to happen and went and borrowed the vessels was the act of faith that caused the miracle to become a reality. This object lesson is for every believer. No matter what it looks like, no matter how impossible it seems, no matter if we are already in the middle of a tragedy – we must do what God tells us to do. In the natural, we will watch God work mightily in our lives. In the spiritual, our capacity to receive the Holy Spirit will be increased by doing all we can humanly do and then we will be filled with His Spirit. Romans 4:19-21 is a fitting scripture to end this lesson. To learn of Christ, is to act in faith when we cannot see the outcome, to act immediately, and to humble ourselves, and to give our all to the end. This is His way. This is His will. This is His love. Consider prayerfully the Father of the faithful as we exit this classroom in preparation for our next instructor.

19 And being not weak in faith, he considered not his own body now dead, when he was about an hundred years old, neither yet the deadness of Sara's womb: 20 He staggered not at the promise of God through unbelief; but was strong in faith, giving glory to God; 21 And being fully persuaded that, what he had promised, he was able also to perform. Romans 4:19-21

Lessons from the Pot of oil:

- Sometimes there is value in "knowing someone who knows someone."
- By Divine adoption we are connected to the Holy Spirit, who is connected to Jesus, who is connected to The Father. We benefit completely from Christ's relationship with the Father.
- Whenever we are facing a trial, no matter how great the adversity, the first question we need to consider is "What hast thou in the house?"
- God often uses that which is overlooked or deemed as insignificant.
- There will be times in our lives when we realize the least likely thing–the thing still hanging around,

the thing we thought we had disposed of long ago–has been saved to be the God-given answer to our problems.

- We must be willing to give and to do our all for God to work mightily on our behalf.

- Oil is a symbol or representation of the Holy Spirit.

- In Scripture, oil is closely associated with anointing, and anointing is closely associated with the Holy Spirit.

- Halfhearted service, halfhearted effort will not produce the vessel prepared for the Holy Spirit.

- Surrender to God requires all our might, our very best. God accepts nothing less.

- Often, God requires a tremendous amount of humility to accomplish a desired request.

- No matter what it looks like, no matter how impossible it seems, no matter if we are already in the middle of a tragedy – we must do what God tells us to do.

- To learn of Christ, is to act in faith when we cannot see the outcome, to act immediately, and to humble ourselves, and to give our all to the end. This is His way. This is His will. This is His love.

The Mustard Seed

Its beginning is not very much, such a tiny little seed,
But placed within this little teacher is all that you will need
To face the battles life indeed will bring right to your door.
Your heart would faint in terror if you knew what was in store
For all who choose to ultimately stand strong for their Saviour,
To show not in their words alone, but display in their behavior,
The attributes that lie within this grain of such small size,
But the mindset that we gain from it is what we realize
Will help us through each trial, it matters not how long.
It matters not how hard it is, how weighty or how strong.
The faith that's like a mustard seed draws power from disdain,
It specializes in growing in an atmosphere of pain.
It doesn't let environment get in the way of growing
By faith in all God's promises it praises Him while knowing
It MUST all work together for your eternal good
And that is why your faith continues growing as it should.

Derek Arthur Sharpe

The Mustard Seed

31 Another parable put he forth unto them, saying, The kingdom of heaven is like to a grain of mustard seed, which a man took, and sowed in his field:
32 Which indeed is the least of all seeds: but when it is grown, it is the greatest among herbs, and becometh a tree, so that the birds of the air come and lodge in the branches thereof. Matthew 13:31-32

20 And Jesus said unto them, Because of your unbelief: for verily I say unto you, If ye have faith as a grain of mustard seed, ye shall say unto this mountain, Remove hence to yonder place; and it shall remove; and nothing shall be impossible unto you.
21 Howbeit this kind goeth not out but by prayer and fasting. Matthew 17:20-21

18 Then said he, Unto what is the kingdom of God like? and whereunto shall I resemble it?

19 It is like a grain of mustard seed, which a man took, and cast into his garden; and it grew, and waxed a great tree; and the fowls of the air lodged in the branches of it. Luke 13:18-19

Our next class will be taught by a tiny instructor with a big message. The teacher for this class is the mustard seed. God has authorized the mustard seed to teach many vital lessons to the body of Christ. It will be our privilege and opportunity to be exposed to a few of them that we may better understand the ways, the will, and the love of Christ, as we are continuing to Learn of Him.

The very first lesson our tiny seed professor would have us embrace is that it matters not how we start off. It's how we end up! The mustard seed is the tiniest of all seeds, but as it relates to plants in a garden, it outgrows them all and towers over them like a tree! There are those who would like to split hairs as to whether a mustard plant is a tree. There are countless accounts on the internet debating whether the Bible was accurate in portraying the mustard seed plant as growing into a tree. Our tiny instructor would direct our attention to Matthew 13:32 which states clearly that it grows to be the greatest of all the herbs. The Bible refers to the mustard plant as an herb and therefore its characterization as a tree points to its comparison to all the other herbs in the garden or in the field. God always knows what He is talking about. It is we that must stay connected to the Spirit so we may gain the correct understanding of what is being taught in the class. But back to the real object at hand. Pay close attention to Ecclesiastes 7:8: *"Better is the end of a thing than the beginning thereof: and the patient in spirit is better than the proud in spirit."* The mustard seed is the champion of the slow start, the small start, the unpromising start. This is an object lesson that all God's people would do well to learn because it teaches us one of the characteristics of God. He prefers to work with small as opposed to big. God told Gideon He could not use a large number because humans tend to take the glory to themselves. Judges 7:2:

And the Lord said unto Gideon, The people that are with thee are too many for me to give the Midianites into their hands, lest Israel vaunt themselves against me, saying, Mine own hand hath saved me.

But God won a mighty victory with just 300 soldiers! God likes dealing with small things. Indeed, the Bible states that God chose Israel even though they were the smallest of all nations because He loved them. That is His way. A mustard seed way!

The Lord did not set his love upon you, nor choose you, because ye were more in number than any people; for ye were the fewest of all people:
8 But because the Lord loved you, and because he would keep the oath which he had sworn unto your fathers, hath the Lord brought you out with a mighty hand, and redeemed you out of the house of bondmen, from the hand of Pharaoh king of Egypt.
Deuteronomy 7:7-8

Our mustard seed instructor assures us that the amount we begin with has nothing to do with what we will end up with OR with what we will be able to accomplish if God is with us and for us.

The next lesson we will learn from the mustard seed is wonderful! It is a lesson on faith. The mustard seed has been honored by the Creator of the universe to be chosen, selected, set aside to represent a tremendous faith principle to the children of God. Please consider prayerfully what our almost microscopic instructor is about to tell us. The Bible states that we should have the faith as a grain of mustard seed. Most individuals gravitate towards the application that all we need is a little faith and we will be able to move mountains. There is a possibility that the Bible itself contradicts that application. Why? Because every time Jesus refers to "little faith," "small faith," or any other characterization that gives the connotation of there not being a great quantity of faith, it is in the negative. Never does Christ commend an individual for having a small amount of faith. Let us consider some examples.

30 Wherefore, if God so clothe the grass of the field, which today is, and tomorrow is cast into the oven, shall he not much more clothe you, O ye of little faith? 31 Therefore take no thought, saying, What shall we eat? or, What shall we drink? or, Wherewithal shall we be clothed? Matthew 6:30-31

And he saith unto them, Why are ye fearful, O ye of little faith? Then he arose, and rebuked the winds and the sea; and there was a great calm. Matthew 8:26

31 And immediately Jesus stretched forth his hand, and caught him, and said unto him, O thou of little faith, wherefore didst thou doubt?
32 And when they were come into the ship, the wind ceased. Matthew 14:31-32

7 And they reasoned among themselves, saying, It is because we have taken no bread.
8 Which when Jesus perceived, he said unto them, O ye of little faith, why reason ye among yourselves, because ye have brought no bread?
9 Do ye not yet understand, neither remember the five loaves of the five thousand, and how many baskets ye took up? Matthew 16:7-9

Even the man who had brought his son to be healed by Jesus, recognized that the amount of faith he possessed was not enough, and therefore his plea to Jesus was, "*Lord I believe, help Thou mine unbelief*" (Mark 9:24). There is one other aspect we must take into consideration as it relates to the concept that "little faith" can do gigantic things. It just does not fit with God's way. We have learned that God's way is a progressive way, a way of stages and phases. Certain abilities come when a person has progressed or attained a certain level of spiritual maturity. The idea that "baby faith" produces "adult results" is not consistent with what is taught in Scripture. In Scripture, the word "great" is used to depict the highest of something, or the pinnacle of a thing. Examples of this concept are as follows:

When Jesus heard it, he marvelled, and said to them that followed, Verily I say unto you, I have not found so great faith, no, not in Israel. Matthew 8:10

Clearly, high level faith.

Great peace have they which love thy law: and nothing shall offend them. Psalms 119:165

Again, clearly a high level of spiritual maturity where nothing bothers or offends.

And God made two great lights; the greater light to rule the day, and the lesser light to rule the night: he made the stars also. Genesis 1:16

The sun and the moon, the most prominent of lights in the sky.

And upon her forehead was a name written, mystery, Babylon the great, the mother of harlots and abomi- nations of the earth. Revelation 17:5

The mother or originator of all harlots – highest.

As good students, in our spare time, we should continue to study for ourselves and we will confirm that "great" in the Bible does indeed symbolize a very high degree of something. We bring this point out because it fits with the following scripture found in 1 Corinthians 13:2 which states:

And though I have the gift of prophecy, and under- stand all mysteries, and all knowledge; and though I have all faith, so that I could remove mountains, and have not charity, I am nothing.

Mountain-moving faith, the same faith that is referenced as "a grain of mustard seed" is referred to as all faith. Does all faith sound like small or little faith? There is another possible application. All and great are used together in the Bible.

And Saul was consenting unto his death. And at that time there was a great persecution against the church which was at Jerusalem; and they were all scattered abroad throughout the regions of Judaea and Samaria, except the apostles. Acts 8:1

What made the persecution great? It scattered all.

And there stood up one of them named Agabus, and signified by the spirit that there should be great dearth throughout all the world: which came to pass in the days of Claudius Caesar. Acts 11:28

Again, what made the dearth or the famine great? It impacted all the world.

And suddenly there was a great earthquake, so that the foundations of the prison were shaken: and immediately all the doors were opened, and every one's bands were loosed. Acts 16:26

How was the greatness of the earthquake measured? Immediately all the doors were opened.

If we continue this study on our own, we will find that all and great are definitely used in conjunction with each other. This leaves us with a question: If mustard seed faith is not small faith, what *is* mustard seed faith? It is all about Him! The scripture does not refer to the size of the mustard seed; it refers to the *nature* of the mustard seed! The mustard seed is resilient. It does not require much care and attention. It can thrive under harsh conditions. It can grow in warm or cool climates and can even thrive though not at its best in hot or cold climates. What is the lesson God is striving to teach us? Mountain-moving faith is faith that cannot be moved! It is faith that can stand and withstand no matter what circumstances and situations present themselves. Mustard seed faith is faith that functions just as well in the coldness of a situation as in the heat of the moment. This is Mustard seed faith. In peace or adversity, mature faith will not be shaken. It is a goal to be attained, not something that a person is just granted at the beginning. Remember God's way? It is a way of progression. As Christians we GROW into that kind of faith. It is a faith that is developed and cultivated.

Galatians 5:22, 23 provides a list of the fruit of the Spirit. One of the fruit of the Spirit is faith. Fruit must develop and mature. Most people do not want to eat the apple seed; they prefer to wait until the seed becomes an apple. We have again learned God's way, God's will, and God's love, through the mustard seed. In His love, God knows just how much faith to expect of us because He and He alone, knows where we are in our journey with Him. He does not place more on us than we can bear (1 Corinthians 10:13). That is even more reason to love Him! Thus, ends another class.

Lessons from the Mustard Seed:

- It matters not how we start off. It's how we end up!
- The mustard seed is the champion of the slow start, the small start, the unpromising start.
- God usually prefers to work with small as opposed to big.
- The concept that "little faith" can do gigantic things does not fit with God's way.

- The idea that "baby faith" produces "adult results" is not consistent with what is taught in Scripture.

- The scripture does not refer to the size of the mustard seed; it refers to the *nature* of the mustard seed.

- The mustard seed is resilient. It does not require much care and attention. It can thrive under harsh conditions.

- Mountain-moving faith is faith that cannot be moved! It is faith that can stand and withstand no matter what circumstances and situations present themselves.

- Mustard seed faith is faith that functions just as well in the coldness of a situation as in the heat of the moment. This is Mustard seed faith. In peace or adversity, mature faith will not be shaken.

- As Christians we GROW into that kind of faith. It is a faith that is developed and cultivated. It is not just granted to us at the beginning.

- God knows just how much faith to expect of us because He and He alone, knows where we are in our journey with Him. He does not place more on us than we can bear.

The Sower

Determined and persistent, unshakeable in His quest.

No matter what, come what may the Sower does His best

To accomplish the Divine mission, to reach the ultimate goal,

To rescue those who would be rescued, to save the perishing soul.

He goes to all kinds of hideouts, He looks midst the high and the low.

No matter the type of environment, there is nowhere
this man will not go.

He has never been known to play favorites, He's not partial,
not even one bit.

He has gone to the worst of all places, just go and so patiently sit,

And wait for the right opportunity and then He produces His seed

And quick as a flash He's accomplished His task to those
with the greatest of need.

He's at home with the rich and the famous, they don't intimidate
Him at all.

He helps them to see, that they need His seed, that He'll be
there whenever they call.

He's not stingy with His precious seed, He sows it everywhere,

But no matter where He sows it, each seed is sown with care.

He wants us all to make it, He'll do whatever He can

To make sure that you blossom and grow, right there in His hand.

Derek Arthur Sharpe

The Sower

3 And he spake many things unto them in parables, saying, Behold, a sower went forth to sow;

4 And when he sowed, some seeds fell by the way side, and the fowls came and devoured them up:

5 Some fell upon stony places, where they had not much earth: and forthwith they sprung up, because they had no deepness of earth:

6 And when the sun was up, they were scorched; and because they had no root, they withered away.

7 And some fell among thorns; and the thorns sprung up, and choked them:

8 But other fell into good ground, and brought forth fruit, some an hundredfold, some sixtyfold, some thirtyfold.

9 Who hath ears to hear, let him hear. Matthew 13:3-9

There are a variety of divine instructors that are located within the Parable of the Sower. Because at this time we are all choosing to major in "Learning of Him," our Heavenly Guidance Counselor has directed us to take the course that is offered by the Sower. Therefore, our next divinely appointed, heavenly authorized, fully accredited and certified instructor is Professor Sower.

Often, we have experienced this parable from the perspective of the different types of soil. We have gained insight from the educator of the good soil, the instructor of the wayside soil, the professor of the stony soil, as well as the teacher of the thorny soil. We, through the aid of the Holy Spirit, have been able to see ourselves in each of these conditions at various stages of our life and we have been blessed by the Divine illumination that has followed. But this time, we will take the focus away from us and place it squarely and completely on the Sower. He will teach us truths, that, if received, will change our lives forever.

The parable begins in a very simple way. "Behold, a Sower went forth to sow." We must not miss the significance of the very first word of the parable, behold—or look, see, watch, understand. When we see the words "behold," "see," "look," "watch" in the Bible, it is important that we comprehend what is being asked of us from God's perspective. It is not just a casual word thrown in to fill space. It is a divinely-inspired, Spirit-led placement of a specific word in a specific place. It is beckoning us, compelling us to pay attention to what is being presented. When we come across the concept of eyes in the Bible, we must learn today that it is God's way of articulating the concept of understanding. Let us consider this principle as it is brought forth in Ephesians 1:18:

The eyes of your understanding being enlightened; that ye may know what is the hope of his calling, and what the riches of the glory of his inheritance in the saints.

Eyes in the Bible represent understanding, or comprehension. In our day-to-day conversation, we even utilize this principle after having said something, we ask "Do you *see* what I am saying?" This concept is also found in other places in the Bible:

"Hear now this, O foolish people, and without understanding; which have eyes, and see not; which have ears, and hear not. Jeremiah 5:21

229

Why were they without understanding? Because they refused to see and hear. The text said they were in possession of eyes and ears, but they did not use them to understand.

We also picked up an additional concept that the ears as it relates to the Bible also represent understanding. We will see this in one more place and that should be sufficient for now:

Therefore speak I to them in parables: because they seeing see not; and hearing they hear not, neither do they understand.

14 And in them is fulfilled the prophecy of Esaias, which saith, By hearing ye shall hear, and shall not understand; and seeing ye shall see, and shall not perceive:

15 For this people's heart is waxed gross, and their ears are dull of hearing, and their eyes they have closed; lest at any time they should see with their eyes, and hear with their ears, and should understand with their heart, and should be converted, and I should heal them.

16 But blessed are your eyes, for they see: and your ears, for they hear. Matthew 13:13-16

If we refuse to understand or do not allow our mindsets to be open to understanding, we cannot be converted.

What a powerful principle!

Now, we have clear understanding that at the very beginning of this parable we are being admonished to understand and the very first concept that we are introduced to is the Sower. What is it that God wants us to learn from the Sower today? Indiscriminate Benevolence. Oh, the grace and mercy of God! The Sower, who represents Christ, did not just sow the seed in the good soil. He did not have the mindset that He would not waste the precious seed on soil that was not in a position to receive it. He did not have the mindset to sow only where the soil was ready. The Bible says that He sowed on all the soils. Today we are going to learn the new phrase our instructor has introduced to us – Indiscriminate Benevolence – Doing good, distributing blessings wherever, whenever, not looking for anything in return, just obeying the promptings of the Holy Spirit. This is Jesus' way. Yes, there are blessings, special blessings, that God reserves for those who are His children, but we must understand this crucial concept. The seed, which is represented as the word of God in Scripture and rightly so, has another deeper application. The seed represents opportunity. The Sower, which is Jesus, distributes the seed (which is the word, which is Jesus) to even the worst of soils that all may have an opportunity to experience eternal life. That is the way of our indiscriminately benevolent Saviour! Everybody gets a chance. Everybody deserves a chance! No matter how wicked, no matter how rebellious, no matter how they have resisted His tender call, He still sows. The Bible states it like this:

"That ye may be the children of your Father which is in heaven: for he maketh his sun to rise on the evil and on the good, and sendeth rain on the just and on the unjust." Matthew 5:45

We need to pause for a moment and consider how good our Heavenly Father and His Son are to the people on this earth! The air we breathe is His air. The atheist, who does not believe in the existence of God, must use God's air and God's life to deny His existence! The infidel, who curses God and does not believe in His will or His ways or His love, must use God's breath, God's air to curse with. And God allows them both to do so. Why? Because both need the air and the life to have the opportunity to one day change their position and their perspective. This is the lesson the Sower teaches us. And lest we believe that only God is expected to possess such wonderfully benevolent and merciful attributes and characteristics, always remember that the reason we are to learn of Him is, so we can, by His grace and power, be like Him. God wants us to allow the Holy Spirit to so control our lives that we give opportunities to the unlovable, the unappreciative, the downright mean and nasty people. Those who have caused us great pain and sorrow – They too, deserve—no, they *need,* an opportunity to allow Jesus into their lives. This is His way. This is His will. This is His love. There is another scripture our Sower teacher would like to leave with us before he teaches us one last principle. It is found in Ecclesiastes 11:1-6. This is additional reiteration of this critical concept that has been presented today.

Cast thy bread upon the waters: for thou shalt find it after many days.
2 Give a portion to seven, and also to eight; for thou knowest not what evil shall be upon the earth.
3 If the clouds be full of rain, they empty themselves upon the earth: and if the tree fall toward the south, or toward the north, in the place where the tree falleth, there it shall be.

4 He that observeth the wind shall not sow; and he that regardeth the clouds shall not reap.

5 As thou knowest not what is the way of the spirit, nor how the bones do grow in the womb of her that is with child: even so thou knowest not the works of God who maketh all.

6 In the morning sow thy seed, and in the evening withhold not thine hand: for thou knowest not whether shall prosper, either this or that, or whether they both shall be alike good.

Cast or sow your bread, or your seed, upon the waters. That represents all waters. (By the way, in scripture, waters represent people. You can find this in Revelation 17:15). Verse 6 shows us that we have been talking about seed all along and finishes up with admonishing us to sow in the morning to catch the early risers and continue to sow in the evening to catch those that we were not able to reach in the morning. It is so hard to fathom the fact that there are those out there in our world today who are choosing not to love a Saviour who is so indiscriminately benevolent. The instructor would like to add something right here just in case there are those who are not completely sure what "indiscriminate" and "benevolent" really mean.

Webster's 1828 Dictionary states -

INDISCRIM'INATE, a. [L. indiscriminatus. See Discriminate.]

1. Undistinguishing; not making any distinction; as the indiscriminate voraciousness of a glutton.

DISCRIMINATE, v.t. [l., difference, distinction; differently applied; Gr., L.]

1. To distinguish; to observe the difference between; as, we may usually discriminate true from false modesty.

2. To separate; to select from others; to make a distinction between; as, in the last judgment, the righteous will be discriminated from the wicked.

3. To mark with notes of difference; to distinguish by some note or mark. We discriminate animals by names, as nature has discriminated them by different shapes and habits.

BENEV'OLENCE, n. [L. benevolentia, of bene, well and volo, to will or wish. See Will.]

1. The disposition to do good; good will; kindness; charitableness; the love, of mankind, accompanied with a desire to promote their happiness.

The benevolence of God is one of his moral attributes; that attribute which delights in the happiness of intelligent beings. "God is love." 1 John 4.

2. An act of kindness; good done; charity given.

BENEV'OLENT, a. [L. benevolens, of bene and volo.]

Having a disposition to do good; possessing love to mankind, and a desire to promote their prosperity and happiness; kind.

So, considering the definitions, the Sower went forth to sow with a mindset not to make any distinction or difference between who He would do good towards, show kindness to, or allow His love to embrace. This is indiscriminate benevolence, and this is who the Sower *is*, not was, and who we will be as we yield to the promptings of the Holy Spirit.

The final lesson from the Sower is His complete and total confidence in the seed. He sowed among all soils because He had confidence that even under the worst conditions and circumstances, some of the seed would make it. The wonderful thing about applying this scenario to people is that the power of God can melt the hardest heart. It can penetrate the darkest mind. It can heal those that are the most sin-sick. The Sower sows everywhere because He knows the power of what He is sowing! We cannot share the love of Jesus with fear and apprehension, with doubt and hesitancy. We too, must have the confidence that no matter how it looks, no matter how long it takes, *somebodies*–and I do mean plural–will accept the Jesus that we are sowing, as long as we have learned of Him to sow it His way, in His will, in His love. Class dismissed.

Lessons from the Sower:

- Eyes in the Bible represent understanding or comprehension.
- If we refuse to understand or do not allow our mindsets to be open to understanding, we cannot be converted.

- The Sower represents Christ.

- Indiscriminate Benevolence is doing good, distributing blessings wherever, whenever, not looking for anything in return, just obeying the promptings of the Holy Spirit.

- In this parable the seed represents not only the word of God, but it also represents opportunity.

- The Sower does not just sow His seed on good soil. He sows His seed on all types of soil.

- It is the will, the way, and the love of Jesus to provide an opportunity for all to be saved no matter how wicked or unlovable.

- God wants us to allow the Holy Spirit to so control our lives that we give opportunities to the unlovable, the unappreciative, the downright mean and nasty people. Those who have caused us great pain and sorrow.

- The Sower has complete and total confidence in the seed.

- The power of God can melt the hardest heart.

- We also must have confidence that the Jesus that we sow in the lives of others will bear fruit.

The Pearl

The only way that I can be is something must be wrong.

There must be irritation, objects where they don't belong.

And then a process is begun, straight from the Master's hand,

It starts with some secretion from a special type of gland.

Only God with all His skill could come up with this way

To turn a problem into a gem, to turn darkness into day.

To make that which is a problem a thing to cause delight.

To transform something that is wrong into something wholly right.

The pearl is not your average gem, no edges, smooth and round

It has a myriad of hues, within it rainbows can be found.

Not brilliant like the diamond, it has not the rubies depth,

But place the pearl within the light and you will catch your breath.

For through the varied colors shines the Master's mighty theme

Even through adversity and in spite of how it may seem,

God does take the thing that's bad and make it completely good,

And cause all who see it to marvel, just like He said He would.

Derek Arthur Sharpe

The Pearl

*45 Again, the kingdom of heaven is like unto a mer-
chant man, seeking goodly pearls:*
*46 Who, when he had found one pearl of great
price, went and sold all that he had, and bought it.*
Matthew 13:45-46

*And the twelve gates were twelve pearls; every
several gate was of one pearl: and the street of the
city was pure gold, as it were transparent glass.*
Revelation 21:21

This class will be conducted by Professor Pearl. As with
all the other instructors that have come before us, this
educator does indeed carry the endorsement of Heaven. At
times, he holds classes at the Educational Institute of Nature.

Today he is holding his class at the Educational Institute of Biblical Knowledge and Understanding. Professor Pearl has several different courses that he teaches, based on Matthew 13: 45, 46. His emphasis today will be on Jesus.

The pearl is a valuable treasure. It is produced in the oyster, one of God's creatures. Our instructor would like for us to grasp a wonderful piece of information before we get into the deep aspects of this precious gem. When the right light shines upon the pearl, the colors of the rainbow are displayed. This aspect of the pearl has great significance. There is a unique quality that the pearl possesses that is not found in many other precious stones. Other stones are known for their brilliance and brightness. When seen in the proper light they shine and sparkle with awe-inspiring beauty. Pearls shine as well, but they shine differently. They are iridescent when they shine. Iridescent means to shine with many different colors when seen from different angles. When the light hits a pearl, the colors of the rainbow are displayed. It recalls the scripture admonition in Matthew 5:16 which tells us to let our light so shine. As Christians we don't want to just shine, we want to *so* shine. It is this iridescent shine that allows more than one aspect of Jesus the light of the world to be seen in our lives. It corresponds so wonderfully with God's love. John 3:16 reminds us that God doesn't just love, He *so* loves. Love is multifaceted, multi-dimensional. There are so many different aspects of the love of God, and the pearl, with its unique ability to capture the colors of the rainbow, has been selected as a heavenly messenger to show God's people how to shine or so shine.

Life always presents us from different angles to others. Sometimes we are seen while we are in adversity. Sometimes we are seen in the midst of great loss. Sometimes we are seen in the midst of overwhelming prosperity and success. The pearl wants us to learn the valuable lesson that no matter what angle a person views us from, we are to so shine. Shine so people see Jesus in us. Our response to the situation provides an opportunity for someone else to see Jesus, so react so that they will! Both in Revelation 4:3 and in Revelation 10:1 we see a rainbow. In one place it surrounds the throne of God; in the other place it surrounds Jesus Himself. This tells us that the rainbow is intimately connected to God, and the pearl, because it displays the rainbow when the light hits it, has been especially selected to display Jesus, different aspects of Jesus, each time it shines. What our pearl instructor wants us to know is that God wants each of us to be pearl instructors as well! What a glorious privilege! What a sacred honor! To be called upon to so shine that various aspects of our Lord and Saviour will be displayed in our lives. That lesson is only secondary to the true reason he has been asked to stand before us today. The word that he wants us to write upon the white boards of our hearts today is adjustment. This is the secret to the iridescent nature of the pearl. The pearl is the fruit of the oyster's reaction to an irritation. When a grain of sand or some other particle finds itself within the soft tissues of the oyster, the oyster does not try to get rid of the irritation. It just makes an adjustment. It secretes a substance that just happens to be called pearl. That substance surrounds that irritation and surrounds that irritation until the irritation is no longer an irritation! The final product of the adjustment is a pearl! When sin entered our beloved earth, the entire planet became irritated. But wonder of wonders, the Father did not respond to the irritation in earth the same way He responded to the irritation in Heaven. When sin entered Heaven, God kicked sin out. But when sin entered the earth, when irritation entered the earth, God didn't kick it out. God sent His son! God sent the Pearl! For thirty-three and a half precious years Jesus, the pearl of great price, wrapped Himself around sin, wrapped Himself around that horrible irritation until at last, while hanging on the cross for our sins, He proclaimed triumphantly, it is finished! The irritation is gone. No matter how we look at it, from whatever vantage point, the pearl so shines! Jesus wrapped Himself around that irritation, that sin for you and me. He didn't just get rid of sin, but the Bible teaches us that he was made sin. Our precious Saviour became sin, so we would not have to pay a price we could not pay! Oh, what precious love!

For he hath made him to be sin for us, who knew no sin; that we might be made the righteousness of God in him. 2 Corinthians 5:21

An inspired writer was impressed to say it in these words:

"Hating sin with a perfect hatred, He yet gathered to His soul the sins of the whole world. Guiltless, He bore the punishment of the guilty. Innocent, yet offering Himself as a substitute for the transgressor. The guilt of every sin pressed its weight upon the divine soul of the world's Redeemer. The evil thoughts, the evil words, the evil deeds of every son and daughter of Adam, called for retribution upon Himself; for He had become man's substitute.

Though the guilt of sin was not His, His spirit was torn and bruised by the transgressions of men, and He who knew no sin became sin for us, that we might be made the righteousness of God in Him. (12)

What a God! What a Friend! What a Saviour! What a Pearl! This was the greatest adjustment ever made. When sin entered this world through the poor decision of Adam, Jesus—who already was a pearl–agreed to be secreted into the world and wrap Himself around sin, even to the point of dying on the cross.

This Heavenly ordained educator always has a life changing class. Every student who has ever taken His course has left with an entirely different outlook and appreciation for what Christ did and who He is. They have a greater appreciation for His will, His way, and His love.

There is one final concept that our instructor would like to share with us before class is dismissed. It is found in the second scripture that opens this classroom–Revelation 21:21.

And the twelve gates were twelve pearls; every several gate was of one pearl: and the street of the city was pure gold, as it were transparent glass.

Our Lord and Saviour could have chosen any precious stone in the world to make the gates of the New Jerusalem. Diamonds, rubies, sapphires, emeralds, even a combination of precious stones, but He chose the pearl. Let us envision the rainbow around every gate, the deep iridescent message proclaimed: God is acknowledging our struggle. Each pearl represents a victory, an irritation overcome! Every child of God will pass through a gate that represents the fact that (1) Jesus Himself, the Pearl of Great price, suffered and surrounded the irritation of sin so that we could enter that gate, and (2) each precious child of God had to learn the lesson of becoming a pearl, so that they too, could allow Jesus to show them how to suffer and struggle and adjust to every trial and tribulation in their life and let Jesus surround it completely with His love!

Twelve gates, each of one gigantic pearl. I can't wait to go in and see the rainbow colors all around that gate. It is going to be glorious! By God's grace, we have been drawn a little closer to our iridescent Saviour. Yes, we can and must apply these precious principles of the pearl to our lives, so that we, by the grace and strength of God, can turn the irritations in our lives into iridescent pearls that will bring others to a deeper love and appreciation for your Jesus. But please never forget that the nature of the pearl, the character of the pearl, the way of the pearl, is His way, His will, His love. The pearl is the oyster's reaction to an irritation. A luminous, iridescent response to an irritation, a rainbow-colored adjustment to an irritation. Rainbows and oysters, who would have ever made the connection? Our Saviour did. It's His way, It's His will, It's His love. Another class has ended. The journey is sweet, but it is not over.

Lessons from the Pearl:

- When the right light shines upon the pearl, the colors of the rainbow are displayed.
- Pearls shine differently from other gems. Pearls shine with iridescence. This means when light hits the pearl from different angles, different colors of the rainbow appear.
- Love is multifaceted, multi-dimensional. There are so many different aspects of the love of God, and the pearl, with its unique ability to capture the colors of the rainbow, has been selected as a heavenly messenger to show God's people how to shine or so shine.

- Life always presents us from different angles to others. It shows us in different situations and circumstances. Some are challenging and trying, some are wonderful.

- The pearl wants us to learn the valuable lesson that no matter what angle a person views us from, we are to so shine.

- We are to shine so people see Jesus in us.

- The rainbow is intimately connected to who God is.

- The pearl is the fruit of the oyster's reaction to an irritation.

- Jesus was sent as the pearl to wrap Himself around the irritation of sin in this world.

- There are 12 gates in the New Jerusalem and each is made of one gigantic pearl.

- Each gate represents Jesus' response to the irritation of sin and each overcomer's response to the trials and tribulations that they had to face to be like Jesus.

The Tare

Insidious in its nature, it exists to mar and mangle.

Its mission is to coexist, to ensnare and to entangle

That which truly is from God, that which should be there,

There is no joy nor gladness when one discovers a tare.

The tare is uninvited, tis not a welcomed guest,

No matter how much work's been done, the tare can make a mess.

Sometimes it's hard to know it's there, difficult to discern,

But there are many lessons from the tare that we can learn.

They enter through a careless door, negligence is the key.

It takes consistent watchfulness or else you will not see

Its silent entrance made while someone was not alert,

The next thing you know, to your dismay, the tare is in the dirt.

Wrapping its roots securely round the precious crop you've sown,

It's goal, to cause anxiety like you have never known.

But praise the Lord, God has a plan for getting all tares out

And that is why in spite of tares, we all can sing and shout.

Derek Arthur Sharpe

The Tare

24 Another parable put he forth unto them, saying, The kingdom of heaven is likened unto a man which sowed good seed in his field:

25 But while men slept, his enemy came and sowed tares among the wheat, and went his way.

26 But when the blade was sprung up, and brought forth fruit, then appeared the tares also.

27 So the servants of the householder came and said unto him, Sir, didst not thou sow good seed in thy field? from whence then hath it tares?

28 He said unto them, An enemy hath done this. The servants said unto him, Wilt thou then that we go and gather them up?

29 But he said, Nay; lest while ye gather up the tares, ye root up also the wheat with them.

30 Let both grow together until the harvest: and in the time of harvest I will say to the reapers, Gather ye together first the tares, and bind them in bundles to burn them: but gather the wheat into my barn.
Matthew 13:24-30

36 Then Jesus sent the multitude away, and went into the house: and his disciples came unto him, saying, Declare unto us the parable of the tares of the field.
37 He answered and said unto them, He that soweth the good seed is the Son of man;
38 The field is the world; the good seed are the children of the kingdom; but the tares are the children of the wicked one;
39 The enemy that sowed them is the devil; the harvest is the end of the world; and the reapers are the angels.
40 As therefore the tares are gathered and burned in the fire; so shall it be in the end of this world.
41 The Son of man shall send forth his angels, and they shall gather out of his kingdom all things that offend, and them which do iniquity;

42 And shall cast them into a furnace of fire: there shall be wailing and gnashing of teeth.
43 Then shall the righteous shine forth as the sun in the kingdom of their Father. Who hath ears to hear, let him hear. Matthew 13:36-43

I t is important that each of us remembers that we have enrolled in the most reputable educational institution in the universe! Its standards are the highest possible and every instructor has been chosen by the Godhead themselves. When we were in the Educational Institute of Nature we sat through a course taught by the thorn, an object in nature that was not created by God but was the result of sin. Here, in the Educational Institute of Biblical Knowledge, we have a similar instructor. Class, I would like to introduce you to the Tare. The tare, unlike the thorn, *is* a part of God's creation, but, as with many things and many people, it has been used by the enemy. For reasons that will not be disclosed at this time, he prefers not to bring attention to the fact that he is an instructor and is, therefore, quite comfortable with just being referred to as the Tare. It is his custom to always begin his class with a definition of his name. It is interesting to note that Matthew 13:24-43 is the only place in the Bible where this term is used and therefore we cannot use the Biblical method of determining the meaning of a word as found in Isaiah 28:9,10 which instructs us:

> 9 *Whom shall he teach knowledge? and whom shall he make to understand doctrine? them that are weaned from the milk, and drawn from the breasts.*
> 10 *For precept must be upon precept, precept upon precept; line upon line, line upon line; here a little, and there a little*:

In most, if not all our other classes, this method of going to various places in the Bible has been implemented. But when there is only a single occurrence of the word, as is the case with the word "tare", we must seek the meaning in its original language and if possible, seek help from a reputable dictionary.

We will first examine the definition of "tare" in the original language from *Strong's Exhaustive Concordance*.

NT:2215
zizanion (dziz-an'-ee-on); of uncertain origin; darnel or false grain:
KJV - tares.

This indicates that the concordance is not aware of the language from which this word comes. The definition in the original appears to be something called "darnel," or false grain.

D'ARNEL, n. A plant of the genus Lolium, a kind of grass; the most remarkable species are the red darnel or rye-grass, and the white darnel.

So, darnel is a species of grass, rye grass to be specific. Not wheat. By the way, the reason our instructor prefers the 1828 dictionary is because Daniel Webster tried to be a Godly man and in his original dictionary, he incorporated scripture definitions whenever possible. All of the instructors prefer to use this dictionary whenever they can. Sometimes it is not possible because the word that is being researched is a word that came into existence after the time period of this dictionary. So, from all we can gather, a tare is rye grass, a false grain, something unwanted and unwelcome in a garden or field of wheat. It is pertinent to note that the Tare's instruction is actually a testimony or witness. This will become clearer as the class progresses. In most places of religious learning this particular parable of our Master is referred to as the Parable of the Wheat and Tares, but in verse 36 of Matthew 13 the disciples give us an entirely different perspective of this parable.

Then Jesus sent the multitude away, and went into the house: and his disciples came unto him, saying, Declare unto us the parable of the tares of the field

The disciples hear this entire parable and they refer to it as "The Tares of the Field." This gives us great insight into this parable, but we will not get sidelined; we will allow The Tare to continue. Our Tare instructor would like us to take note the environment that introduces him. He must also point out that he is being used by the enemy. The Bible says that it was nighttime, and everyone was asleep. It is an extremely important point of the lesson to realize that the implied message in this parable was that someone was asleep on the job! Somehow, everyone knew this was a common practice and when a field had been newly planted, someone was supposed to be on guard at all times until the wheat had reached a level of maturity that would make it immune to the tares. Why is this point so important? Because we are "learning of Him" and the householder is a representation of Jesus. The point is, although the field has suffered a major setback because of someone's negligence and irresponsibility, the householder does not get upset or fire anyone. This is the patience and longsuffering of Jesus. It is His way.

We must note this is not an overnight process. A considerable amount of time has elapsed while the wheat and tares are taking root. Then, they have to break the surface of the earth and bring forth fruit, and then individuals can realize there is more than wheat in the garden. The workers (including the one or ones who were asleep and allowed this situation) are ready to go and pull up all the tares. They are waiting for the householder to give them the "go" sign. Once again, we see the attributes of Jesus shining through. It is not His way to act hastily, impulsively, or emotionally. In patient wisdom that comes from experience and knowledge, He commands the workers to wait. His reason, in their zeal to get to the tares, they will uproot some precious wheat as well. Thus, the declaration: "Let both grow together until harvest." So, we are just going to allow the enemy to stay in the camp and we are not going to do anything about it? An overzealous worker is a dangerous thing in a field of wheat and tares. One grain of wheat lost was too much for the householder to risk. This is a classic example of the age-old adage "time will tell." But here is where our Tare instructor's instruction/testimony takes on a tone of wonder and awe. Do you know how we were treated? Even though we were tares? *Everything* that the wheat received, the householder made sure we received it as well. If they received a special fertilizer, we received the same fertilizer. When the wheat received water, we, the tares, received just as much water as the wheat. The patience and wisdom of the householder was and is unbelievable. He just waited and waited and waited. We later found out that this was the exact method He used with Judas on earth and with the great enemy in heaven. It must be reiterated that it just is not the way of the Saviour and therefore should not be the way of His children to act rashly, hastily, or upon impulse. Proverbs 3:5, 6 is an excellent admonition right about now. It states

> *5 "Trust in the Lord with all thine heart; and lean not unto thine own understanding.*
> *6 In all thy ways acknowledge him, and he shall direct thy paths."*

Proverbs 29:20 states it another way and it is important to remember Matthew 12:34 and Proverbs 23:7 as well.

"Seest thou a man that is hasty in his words? there is more hope of a fool than of him."Proverbs 29:20

"O generation of vipers, how can ye, being evil, speak good things? for out of the abundance of the heart the mouth speaketh."Matthew 12:34

"For as he thinketh in his heart, so is he: Eat and drink, saith he to thee; but his heart is not with thee." Proverbs 23:7

There is little hope for a man that is hasty in his words. A person's words are an indication of what is in his heart, and finally, what is in his heart is a good barometer for who and how that person actually is. Therefore, the person who is hasty in speech is more than likely a hasty person in most areas of their life and will not be able to emulate or copy the wonderful, patient and wise pattern of the householder, our Lord and Saviour Jesus Christ. A person cannot display the patience and wisdom of Jesus without getting to know Him and allowing Him to control his life. God has an abundance of blessings. He cannot run out. Therefore, it does not trouble Him at all to pour His general blessings upon those who do not even follow Him. To bless those who do not appreciate, nor acknowledge, or even accept His blessings, is – His way, His will, and His love. We end with Matthew 5:45-48.

> *45 That ye may be the children of your Father which is in heaven: for he maketh his sun to rise on the evil and on the good, and sendeth rain on the just and on the unjust.*
> *46 For if ye love them which love you, what reward have ye? do not even the publicans the same?*
> *47 And if ye salute your brethren only, what do ye more than others? do not even the publicans so?*
> *48 Be ye therefore perfect, even as your Father which is in heaven is perfect.*

To be His children, to be like Him, to strive for perfection, is to treat those who are unkind, undeserving, and unlovable with the same kindness you treat those you do love. This is His way, His will, and His love. Take a short break and we will proceed to the next class.

Lessons from the Tare:

- The tare is a part of God's creation, but as with many people, it has been used by the enemy.
- Combining the original language definition with Webster's 1828 dictionary reveals that a tare is rye grass also referred to as a false grain.
- In this parable, tares were sown while someone was sleeping when they should have been watching or guarding.
- Although the field has suffered a major setback because of someone's negligence and irresponsibility, the householder does not get upset or fire anyone. This is the patience and longsuffering of Jesus. It is His way.
- It is not Christ's way to act hastily, impulsively, or emotionally.
- There is little hope for a man that is hasty in his words.
- A person's words are an indication of what is in his heart.
- What is in a person's heart is a good barometer for who and how that person actually is.

- To be His children, to be like Him, to strive for per-fection, is to treat those who are unkind, undeserving, and unlovable with the same kindness you treat those you do love. This is His way, His will, and His love.

The Hidden Treasure

What can cause a man who's sane to relinquish all he possesses?
To pursue a course that normally would be filled with keen distresses.

It makes no sense to those looking on, it has no rhyme or reason.
It cannot be followed, nor figured out, it's completely out of season.

It appears to all who know him well that he's clearly lost his mind,
But oh, if they only knew the joy, what God did help him find.
Yes, he sold all that he had, and bought a piece of land,
No matter what they thought of him, that no one could understand,
He knew what was beneath that dirt, buried safe and sure.
The hidden treasure that had cost him all now makes him quite secure.
God sees us as hidden treasure, He gave His all for YOU.
And now He asked each one of us to do what we saw Him do.
It will be worth it, you will see, for you, there'll be no doubt.
The Hidden treasure in your possession will truly make you shout.
Total surrender, give all for Him, hold back not anything,
And feel the joy, unspeakable bliss that full salvation brings.

Derek Arthur Sharpe

The Hidden Treasure

Again, the kingdom of heaven is like unto treasure hid in a field; the which when a man hath found, he hideth, and for joy thereof goeth and selleth all that he hath, and buyeth that field. Matthew 13:44

Our instructor for this class is found in several places in scripture. The Master has seen fit to use her in many different scenarios and circumstances and I am sure you will be blessed by her presentation. Of course, she is fully endorsed by Heaven and actually has more than one Divine authorization to teach and instruct. Class, please give your prayerful and undivided attention to Hidden Treasure.

The very first thing Hidden Treasure would like to have you learn is that you do not have to say a lot to say a lot. This parable is only one verse long! Thirty-seven words! But it is full to the brim with powerful truths. Our Saviour does not have to use a lot of words to get His point across. In fact, there is a place in our textbook that will tell us that in certain scenarios and circumstances, the more words we use, the greater the opportunity for the enemy to come in and make a mess of things. Let us consider Proverbs 10:19:

> *In the multitude of words there wanteth not sin: but he that refraineth his lips is wise.*

"Wanteth" means to lack, to not have enough of, to be insufficient. That is why Psalms 23:1 is a declaration that every child of God can and should recite each and every day, ESPECIALLY when we are going through times of need. The Bible says, *"The Lord is my shepherd; I shall not want."*

That bears repeating: The Lord is my Shepherd; I shall not want. The definition of want is to lack, to not have enough of, to be insufficient! Now we see why Hidden Treasure was so excited about taking us to this scripture. The children of God confidently declare that because the Lord is their shepherd, every *need*, not desire, not what we think need, but everything we truly and genuinely need, He has to provide, or He would not be a faithful Shepherd. To make sure all our needs are provided for is His way, His will, and His love.

I imagine that some of us are uncertain and not completely convinced. Some of us are in a state of disbelief about this biblical fact and truth about the Good Shepherd. Let us consider this scenario: Your car breaks down and you don't have any other transportation to work. You're forced to depend upon a neighbor to take you to work every day. Does that mean God is not providing your need? Is it possible the Lord orchestrated this mishap, so you can be a blessing to your neighbor? Should you complain, or should you ask God to show you what He wants you to reveal to your neighbor about Him? When your assignment with your neighbor is done, your car will either be fixed miraculously, or you will somehow be provided with another vehicle. That also is His way, His will, and His love. The faith we must have in our loving Shepherd is to know that He only does or allows that which is for our good. We should all practice making a Psalms 23:1 declaration until it is imprinted on our souls.

Let us return to Proverbs 10:19: *In the multitude of words there wanteth not sin: but he that refraineth his lips is wise.*

Now that we know want means lack, this is a powerful lesson. Where there are a lot of words, there is no lack of sin. That is a sobering thought! No wonder we have been admonished to let our "yea be yea and or nay be nay." *But let your communication be, Yea, yea; Nay, nay: for whatsoever is more than these cometh of evil*. Matthew 5:37

We learned all of this just because the verse is short? But what is the lesson from the treasure itself? Well, the first thing we want to learn is that God does not place His really, valuable things where they can be easily found. If it is truly important, truly valuable, then you are going to have to truly hunt, search, inconvenience yourself, or go without to find it, to get it, even sometimes to understand it. Why would the Saviour make the really valuable things so hard to obtain? It weeds out those who are not truly invested. The half-hearted, never-really-cared-that-much-about-it-in-the-first -place individuals are not the ones who will sincerely and genuinely appreciate the special treasures the Saviour has prepared for His children. They would treat them carelessly and end up tossing them aside before long. That is why it must take everything we have to find the treasure. Jeremiah presents it thusly:

And ye shall seek me, and find me, when ye shall search for me with all your heart. Jeremiah 29:13

This is the entire message of the Hidden Treasure. We must give our all. We must want it more than anything in the entire world, even to the point of selling everything we have just to get it! The Saviour places a very high regard on determination and not giving up.

Hidden Treasure wants to teach us this lesson using prayer as an example. This is a lesson that will take our breath away:

And it came to pass, that, as he was praying in a certain place, when he ceased, one of his disciples said unto him, Lord, teach us to pray, as John also taught his disciples.

2 And he said unto them, When ye pray, say, Our Father which art in heaven, Hallowed be thy name. Thy kingdom come. Thy will be done, as in heaven, so in earth.

3 Give us day by day our daily bread.

4 And forgive us our sins; for we also forgive every one that is indebted to us. And lead us not into temp-tation; but deliver us from evil.

5 And he said unto them, Which of you shall have a friend, and shall go unto him at midnight, and say unto him, Friend, lend me three loaves;

6 For a friend of mine in his journey is come to me, and I have nothing to set before him?

7 And he from within shall answer and say, Trouble me not: the door is now shut, and my children are with me in bed; I cannot rise and give thee.

8 I say unto you, Though he will not rise and give him, because he is his friend, yet because of his importunity he will rise and give him as many as he needeth.

9 And I say unto you, Ask, and it shall be given you; seek, and ye shall find; knock, and it shall be opened unto you.

10 For every one that asketh receiveth; and he that seeketh findeth; and to him that knocketh it shall be opened. Luke 11:1-10

These verses delineate a prayer principle. When God tells you" no," you are supposed to keep asking until He tells you yes. What is that Hidden Treasure is saying? There is another place in scripture that says this as well.

And he spake a parable unto them to this end, that men ought always to pray, and not to faint;

2 Saying, There was in a city a judge, which feared not God, neither regarded man:

3 And there was a widow in that city; and she came unto him, saying, Avenge me of mine adversary.

4 And he would not for a while: but afterward he said within himself, Though I fear not God, nor regard man;

5 Yet because this widow troubleth me, I will avenge her, lest by her continual coming she weary me.

6 And the Lord said, Hear what the unjust judge saith.

7 And shall not God avenge his own elect, which cry day and night unto him, though he bear long with them?

8 I tell you that he will avenge them speedily. Nevertheless when the Son of man cometh, shall he find faith on the earth? Luke 18:1-8

Luke 18 provides a clearer understanding. The word in Luke 11 was" importunity." Luke 18 defined that for us as "continual coming." Both scripture passages offered specific instructions on how to pray and the message that was loud and clear was "don't take no for an answer." It is that mindset that will not stop until we have obtained the treasure! There is more. The Bible gives a classic example of a woman who had a need and would not allow Jesus to tell her no:

22 And, behold, a woman of Canaan came out of the same coasts, and cried unto him, saying, Have mercy on me, O Lord, thou Son of David; my daughter is grievously vexed with a devil.

23 But he answered her not a word. And his disciples came and besought him, saying, Send her away; for she crieth after us.

24 But he answered and said, I am not sent but unto the lost sheep of the house of Israel.

25 Then came she and worshipped him, saying, Lord, help me.

26 But he answered and said, It is not meet to take the children's bread, and to cast it to dogs.

27 And she said, Truth, Lord: yet the dogs eat of the crumbs which fall from their masters' table.

28 Then Jesus answered and said unto her, O woman, great is thy faith: be it unto thee even as thou wilt.

And her daughter was made whole from that very hour. Matthew 15:22-28

Did we catch all the no's? The woman's request is respectful in verse 22. There were absolutely no problems with her approach, but Jesus ignored her. Some of us realize that to be ignored is sometimes worse than being answered in the negative! That is NO number one. His disciples, completely misreading the lesson Jesus is trying to teach them about their prejudice towards those not of their nation (she was not a Jew) picked up His ignoring her and in her presence and hearing, told the Master to tell her to leave. That's NO number two. Let's recap just for a moment. She asked Jesus respectfully to heal her daughter and He ignores her. She doesn't get mad and leave. His disciples–true, sincere, Heaven ordained, handpicked by the Master–tell the Master to get rid of her. She doesn't get mad and leave.

Let's continue with the story. After the disciples have said that she is not welcome, Jesus speaks. What does He say? He only does miracles for the Jews? What? She doesn't qualify! She's the wrong nationality! This is unbelievable. All this way just to hear she doesn't qualify, through something that isn't her fault and there is absolutely nothing she can do about it? That is a crushing no. Surely, she is going to go back home dejected and discouraged. Who would blame her? But what does she do? The Bible says after three horrible NO's, she comes and worships Him and asks Him again to help her. What was that word again in Luke 11? Importunity, continual coming! Talk about not giving up!

Maybe you were not even aware this was in the Bible! Surely Christ said yes. The next verse says Jesus tells her that the bread He has isn't for the dogs! Wait. First, she gets ignored. Then, the disciples try to get rid of her. Then Jesus tells her she doesn't qualify and now, he calls her a dog!

That's four No's and they keep getting more and more offensive. What in the world can her response be? The most classic example of wisdom and the tongue of the learned in the Bible. She said Truth Lord. What? You are the Lord of Heaven and Earth. You are the Sovereign of the Universe. You can do anything, which includes healing my little girl, so if you want to call me a dog, I will be a dog. But I don't need a loaf of bread, I don't need a slice of bread. I have such complete faith in Your power that if you would just let me sit under the table—like a dog—just one crumb will heal my daughter. This woman was after the *hidden treasure* and would not take NO for an answer! Of course, Jesus healed her daughter. He rewarded her faith. He knew He could trust her to withstand the no's while he taught His disciples how wrong they were to think that just because she was not a Jew, she did not qualify for His help. It is His way, it is His will, it is His love to abundantly reward those who sacrifice all to get to Him.

Before this class ends Hidden Treasure would like to answer the question that is always asked when she teaches the point that the Bible is clear that God *does* say no—"so what do we do with that fact?" God is too kind and merciful to string anyone along for an extremely long time just to tell them that the answer really was "no" after all. That would be cruel. If Jesus says keep on asking Him, even after He has told you no then keep asking Him. Let's put it another way. The key in praying when you hear NO is to keep praying until you hear Christ tell you, 'Don't ask me anymore. The answer really is no." Scripture tells us that God is merciful, and He will not allow anyone to ask more than two or three times maximum before He says "It really is no, Don't ask me anymore." Let's look at what Scripture says:

25 I pray thee, let me go over, and see the good land that is beyond Jordan, that goodly mountain, and Lebanon.

26 But the Lord was wroth with me for your sakes, and would not hear me: and the Lord said unto me, Let it suffice thee; speak no more unto me of this matter. Deuteronomy 3:25-26

Moses had struck the rock when God told him to speak to it, and as a result, he was not allowed to enter the Promised land. Moses tried to beg the Lord to reconsider and God said, "don't ask me anymore."

8 For this thing I besought the Lord thrice, that it might depart from me.

9 And he said unto me, My grace is sufficient for thee: for my strength is made perfect in weakness. Most gladly therefore will I rather glory in my infir- mities, that the power of Christ may rest upon me. 2 Corinthians 12:8-9

Paul had a thorn in the flesh and asked God three times to remove it. But God said, I am not going to remove it. Don't ask Me anymore. My grace will get you through it. As we learn of Him, we see He is fair; He is compassionate; He is considerate. He will not string us along. Until we hear "don't ask Me anymore" –no matter how long it's been –we are to keep asking. We must give our all to get the treasure. Why? Because we are the treasure! And God gave everything He had to get to us. That is His way, That is His will, That is His love, for us. One more class to go.

Lessons from the Hidden Treasure:

- You do not have to say a lot to say a lot.
- Our Saviour does not have to use a lot of words to get His point across.
- In many instances, the more that is said the greater the chance for the enemy to use what is being said.
- It is impossible for a child of God to truly lack because God is a faithful shepherd.
- The faith we must have in our loving Shepherd is to know that He only does or allows that which is for our good.
- God does not place His really, valuable things where they can be easily found.

- The difficulty in finding the treasure weeds out the half hearted who really don't appreciate the treasure as they should.

- The Saviour places a very high regard on determination and not giving up.

- When God tells you "no", you are supposed to keep asking until He tells you yes.

- It is His way, it is His will, it is His love to abundantly reward those who sacrifice all to get to Him.

- We must give our everything to get to God because God gave His everything to get to us.

The Net

The net is quite benevolent, it gives everyone a chance.
No matter what your station, with Christ you can advance.
He'll catch you in His net of love and make you all brand new,
It's nothing short of a miracle, what God will do for you.
You may be small you may be large, or just average is your size.
With God you'll be extraordinary, more than you can ever realize.
This net it catches good and bad, it brings them all to shore,
Gives all the opportunity to be so very much more.
But some unfortunately, will not accept His grace,
They're uncomfortable in His presence, they feel so out of place.
He does not force not one to stay, that's simply not His way.
It must be love and adoration that compels us to obey.
And so, He throws some fish back in, to be eternally lost,
Because they would not appreciate just what salvation cost.
So, decide right now to rest within the Father's tender love,
And He will rain His blessings down on you from Heaven above.

Derek Arthur Sharpe

The Net

Matthew 13:47-50

47 Again, the kingdom of heaven is like unto a net, that was cast into the sea, and gathered of every kind:
48 Which, when it was full, they drew to shore, and sat down, and gathered the good into vessels, but cast the bad away.
49 So shall it be at the end of the world: the angels shall come forth, and sever the wicked from among the just,
50 And shall cast them into the furnace of fire: there shall be wailing and gnashing of teeth.

This is our final course. We have learned so much about our Saviour. We should be happy about our decision to accept the Saviour's invitation to learn of Him. It is time for our last instructor. Our final Heaven-approved, Divinely ordained and accredited Instructor is the Net. . . This is a sobering class. It is of the greatest importance. The Net has been chosen by the Heavenly Guidance Counselor to be the last presentation because it does indeed teach us the way of the Saviour, and at the same time, places your entire life in a different perspective.

The net is a device, in this context, used to catch fish, lots of fish. The more fish the better. This differs greatly from the leisurely concept of sitting on a bank with a rod and reel and waiting for a bite. Fishing with a net is work, strenuous, back-breaking work. One of the most important concepts that we must digest is that whoever is fishing with this particular net is not looking to catch any particular fish. The net catches fish of every kind. That is so encouraging because from the parable we understand that this is a Gospel Net. This is a parable about the Kingdom of God and how it functions, which means it is a parable about how Jesus functions, and therefore allows us to learn something else about His way, His will, and His love. What is the POWER point that Professor Net is emphasizing? Anyone has the opportunity to be caught by Jesus in His gospel net! Let us take a look at how it's worded in John 3:16:

For God so loved the world, that he gave his only begotten Son, that whosoever believeth in him should not perish, but have everlasting life.

The operative word in this wonderful text is *whosoever*! Not just rich people, not just people with a degree, not just people who have never gone to jail, not just people who have never struggled with substance abuse, not just people who have rightfully or wrongfully contracted a social disease. Whosoever means *anybody*. As long as we believe, the OPPORTUNITY for salvation is open to us. That is the way of the Saviour!

All we have to do is study the type of individuals He chose to begin His Christian Church. It is so very encouraging! Thomas was a doubter—he had no faith even though his closest companions for the last three and a half years were assuring him Jesus had risen from the dead (John 20:19-29). Matthew was a top of the line, lowest of the low, steal and extort from his own people tax collector; he was also known as a publican, which in the Bible meant his sin was public knowledge and he didn't care (Matthew 9:9-11). James and John were nicknamed by Jesus the sons of thunder and actually asked Jesus if they could call down fire from heaven and destroy an entire city just because they didn't want to hear from Jesus (Matthew 3:17, Luke 9:52-54). Phillip was a slow learner (John 14:8,9). Of course, we know that Peter denied that he ever knew Jesus, (in Jesus' presence, when Jesus needed Him most (Matthew 26:69-75). And we don't even need to go to scripture regarding Judas. The disciples were a messed up, dysfunctional, fighting-for-greatest-in Christ's-kingdom (Mark 9:34) bunch of individuals. But because Jesus saw something in them that was worth saving, He hung in there with them until they got it right. That over-whelming love is His way. If there is something in us worth saving, then we are worth waiting for, no matter how long it takes. That is His way, His will, and His love.

But now for the sobering side of the class that Instructor Net has been asked to convey. Although the parable clearly states that the net can and does catch every kind of fish, every fish doesn't get to stay. The parable says some fish got thrown back out. Wait a minute. This means we can go to Jesus, be accepted by Jesus, spend a considerable amount of time with Jesus, and still not make it? We told you this class was sobering. Remember Judas? He made the cut. When there were a lot of disciples at first and then it went down to 12, Judas actually stayed (John 6:47-71). But when it was all said and done, his true colors were revealed. He had not allowed Jesus to have all of Him and therefore he did not have what it took to stay with Jesus to the end.

Jesus makes it very clear. We will have to endure some hard times if we want to be with Him. There is no fine print with Jesus. No hidden clauses in the contract. He tells us everything up front in very clear wording. That too, is His way, His will, and His love. He is not a bait and switch God!

These things I have spoken unto you, that in me ye might have peace. In the world ye shall have tribulation: but be of good cheer; I have overcome the world. John 16:33

Notice the scripture doesn't say we "might" have tribulation. Tribulation is a guarantee.

Yea, and all that will live godly in Christ Jesus shall suffer persecution.2 Timothy 3:12

The two operative words in this text are" yes" and "shall." No doubt about it.

9 Then shall they deliver you up to be afflicted, and shall kill you: and ye shall be hated of all nations for my name's sake.

10 And then shall many be offended, and shall betray one another, and shall hate one another.

11 And many false prophets shall rise, and shall deceive many.

12 And because iniquity shall abound, the love of many shall wax cold.

13 But he that shall endure unto the end, the same shall be saved. Matthew 24:9-13

That was serious! But Jesus assures us, if we hang in there, we will make it.

18 If the world hate you, ye know that it hated me before it hated you.

19 If ye were of the world, the world would love his own: but because ye are not of the world, but I have chosen you out of the world, therefore the world hateth you.

20 Remember the word that I said unto you, The servant is not greater than his lord. If they have persecuted me, they will also persecute you; if they have kept my saying, they will keep yours also. John 15:18-20

That was clear. If they hated Jesus, and we act like Jesus, then the world is going to hate us too. That makes sense. That is reasonable. We should be glad that Jesus is upfront in informing us that being a Christian is not a walk in the park. He is an open God. He is an honest God. And most importantly, He is a God who will never leave nor forsake us as long as we want Him in our lives (Hebrews 13:5, Matthew 28:19,20).

This is not a once saved, always saved kind of arrangement. Our getting in doesn't guarantee our staying in. The Bible teaches that there is going to be a judgment. We will be judged based upon the life we have lived, the choices we have made. The net teaches that we could be a powerful instrument in the hand of God to bring many, many people "to the net" and then not actually make it ourselves. 1 Corinthians 9:26, 27 clarifies this point:

26 I therefore so run, not as uncertainly; so fight I, not as one that beateth the air:
27 But I keep under my body, and bring it into subjection: lest that by any means, when I have preached to others, I myself should be a castaway.

Paul was the third most powerful person in the entire New Testament. If he–after all the powerful work he had done, all the many souls he had won for Christ–could still be cast away, then there is definitely not a once saved, always saved kind or arrangement.

Paul was definitely making a reference to Matthew 13:48 which says "cast the bad away."

Paul underscores the reality that even mighty men of God must keep pressing towards the mark or they will fail at making it to the end.

I protest by your rejoicing which I have in Christ Jesus our Lord, I die daily. 1 Corinthians 15:31

The way Paul made it through his Christian journey was to die to self every day. That is not just a "Paul solution." He got that counsel from the Saviour. Consider what Luke 9:23 tells us about staying in the net.

And he said to them all, If any man will come after me, let him deny himself, and take up his cross daily, and follow me.

Crosses are instruments of death. A daily cross is a daily death. This is how Jesus made it for thirty-three and a half years! He died to self each and every day, so we would have the opportunity to live with Him forever. We are going to be judged on just how well we learned of Him.

Let us hear the conclusion of the whole matter: Fear God, and keep his commandments: for this is the whole duty of man.

14 For God shall bring every work into judgment, with every secret thing, whether it be good, or whether it be evil. Ecclesiastes 12: 13, 14

Solomon said that was "the conclusion of the whole matter." The summation of life. We should do right because we will be judged. It is so important that each of us gets thoroughly checked out because God loves us so much that He doesn't want any of us to ever have to experience the sorrows and pain of sin ever again throughout the ceaseless ages of eternity. If we one day down the road turn on Him and bring all these sin problems back and make life miserable again, just like Lucifer did, we will be "thrown back" or "cast away" just so we will never have to worry about sin coming back a second time. That is His way. That is His will. That is His love.

The lesson of the net is we have to hang in there, endure to the end, to be saved, to stay in the net. But the good news is, Jesus does all the hanging in there for us, if we just let Him show us how to fight the good fight of faith (1 Timothy 6:12).

Here are the final four promises that Jesus always tells Professor Net to end the class with. They show us His power. They show us our power when we are with Him. Let us consider the final four scriptures for this our final course.

And Jesus looking upon them saith, With men it is impossible, but not with God: for with God all things are possible. Mark 10:27

I can do all things through Christ which strengtheneth me. Philippians 4:13

But he that shall endure unto the end, the same shall be saved. Matthew 24:13

I am crucified with Christ: nevertheless I live; yet not I, but Christ liveth in me: and the life which I now live in the flesh I live by the faith of the Son of God, who loved me, and gave himself for me. Galatians 2:20

Jesus Himself provides us all the help we need to stay in the net! When we are judged, it is based on *His life, not ours.* That is His way, That is His will, That is His love! We have learned of Him.

Now it is the fervent prayer of each instructor that has taught us on this journey that we will choose to live for Him and stay with Him, by His grace and in His strength. . . . . FOREVER.

This course is completed. Class dismissed!

Lessons from the Net:

- Fishing with a net is work, strenuous, back-breaking work.
- Whoever is fishing with this particular net is not looking to catch any particular fish. The net catches fish of every kind.
- Anyone has the opportunity to be caught by Jesus in His gospel net!
- If there is something in us worth saving, then we are worth waiting for, no matter how long it takes. That is His way, His will, and His love.
- Jesus makes it very clear. We will have to endure some hard times if we want to be with Him. There is no fine print with Jesus. No hidden clauses in the contract. He tells us everything up front in very clear wording. That too, is His way, His will, and His love. He is not a bait and switch God!
- If they hated Jesus, and we act like Jesus, then the world is going to hate us too.

- This is not a once saved, always saved kind of arrangement. Our getting in doesn't guarantee our staying in.

- Even mighty men of God must keep pressing towards the mark or they will fail at making it to the end.

- Crosses are instruments of death. A daily cross is a daily death. This is how Jesus made it for thirty-three and a half years! He died to self each and every day, so we would have the opportunity to live with Him forever.

- The lesson of the net is we have to hang in there, endure to the end, to be saved, to stay in the net. But the good news is, Jesus does all the hanging in there for us, if we just let Him show us how to fight the good fight of faith.

- Jesus Himself provides us all the help we need to stay in the net! When we are judged, it is based on *His life, not ours*. That is His way, That is His will, That is His love!

Bibliography

(1) Meriam Webster online dictionary

(2) Grammarist

(3) Testimonies to the church, Volume 6, p. 186, Ellen White

(4) Wikipedia - Thorns

(5) Fundamentals of Education p.61, Ellen White

(6) The Desire of Ages, p. 173, Ellen White

(7) The Great Controversy, p. 66, Ellen White

(8) Wikipedia, Nests

(9) Christ's Object Lessons, p. 333, Ellen White

(10) Nawinter.com, Soaring

(11) Reflecting Christ, p.282, Ellen White

(12) 1 Selected Messages, p. 321, Ellen White

CPSIA information can be obtained
at www.ICGtesting.com
Printed in the USA
LVHW020728301219
642043LV00002B/146/P